TEACH YOURSELF TO PLAY
GUITAR
SONGS

To access online content visit:
www.halleonard.com/mylibrary
Enter Code
4561-3283-3736-5331

ISBN 978-1-4950-4948-4

HAL•LEONARD®
CORPORATION
7777 W. BLUEMOUND RD. P.O. BOX 13819 MILWAUKEE, WI 53213

Visit Hal Leonard Online at
www.halleonard.com

CONTENTS

BORN UNDER A BAD SIGN
Albert King

Video Lesson – 14 minutes, 53 seconds

Drop D Tuning, Down 1 ½ steps: (low to high)
B–F#–B–E–G#–C#
Key of E (actual song sounds in key of C#)

Guitar Tone:

- light distortion
- light reverb
- bridge pickup
- EQ: bass – 5, mid – 5, treble – 8

Scales:

E Minor Pentatonic Scale

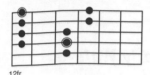

12fr

Techniques:

- String Bending: as in most blues, string bending is a must-know technique. Be sure to keep your bend pitches in tune! Practice these by fretting the target pitches first to hear how far you should bend the strings to nail the proper pitches. Make sure you use some support fingers behind the fretted note.

- Two-Step Bends: during the Guitar Solo, you'll see some two-step bends. You really have to push these up high to get a full two steps. The drop tuning will help as the strings will be looser. It might feel like you're going to break the string, but keep pushing with support fingers behind to get to the correct pitch.

- Vibrato: defined as a repeated fluctuation of pitch, vibrato is typically used on notes of a longer duration. It is achieved by bending and releasing a string over and over. Bent notes are also treated with vibrato. First, bend the note to the desired pitch, then subtly shake the string from this point (slightly bending above and/ or below the position of the bent note).

- Staccato: notes or chords with a dot over them indicate staccato. This means they should be cut short and not allowed to ring out. After the initial attack, use your left and right hands to mute the strings.

Born Under a Bad Sign

Words and Music by Booker T. Jones and William Bell

Drop D tuning, down 1 1/2 steps:
(low to high) B-F#-B-E-G#-C#

Intro
Moderate Blues ♩ = 92

N.C.   C#7

*(E7)

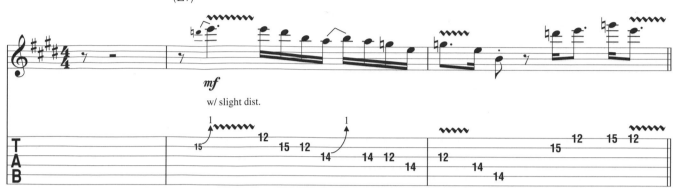

*Symbols in parentheses represent chord names respective to detuned guitar.
Symbols above reflect actual sounding chords. Chord symbols reflect overall harmony.

Chorus
Gtr. tacet

C#7

(E7)

Born _ un-der a bad __ sign.   Been down _ since I be-

G#7

(B7)

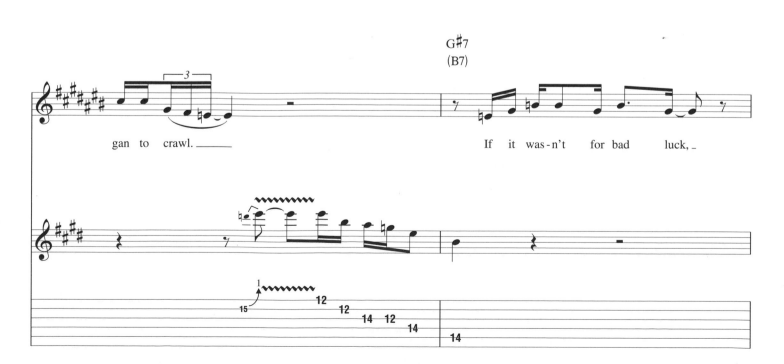

gan to crawl. _____   If it was-n't for bad   luck, _

you know I would-n't have _____ no luck at all.

Verse

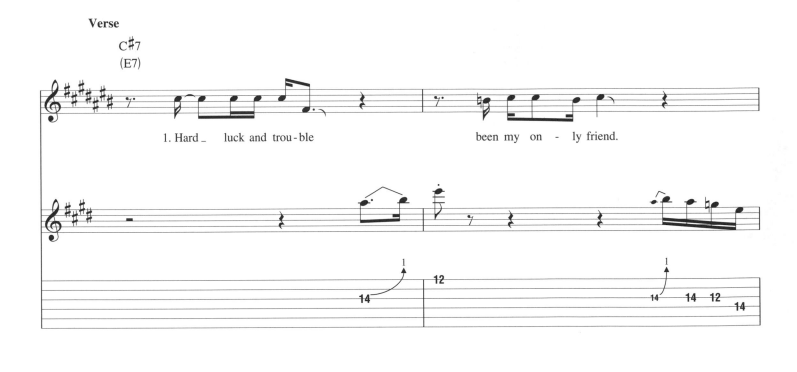

1. Hard _ luck and trou-ble been my on - ly friend.

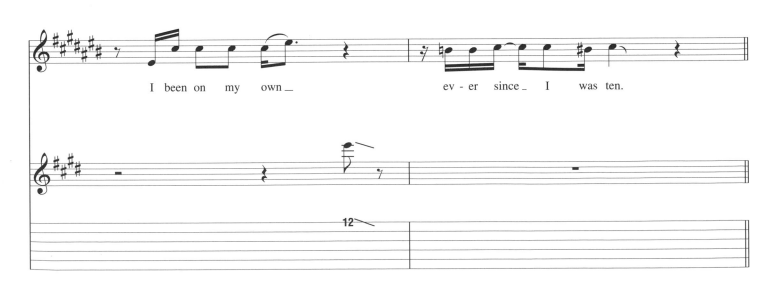

I been on my own _ ev - er since _ I was ten.

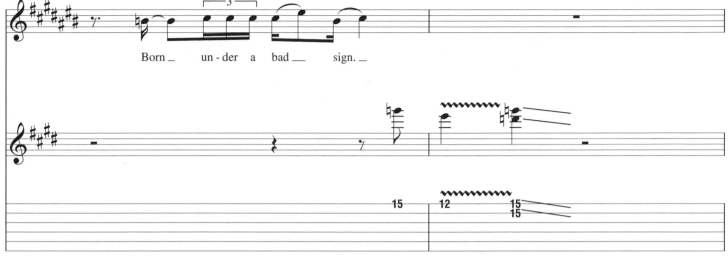

C#7
(E7)

Born _ un - der a bad _ sign. _

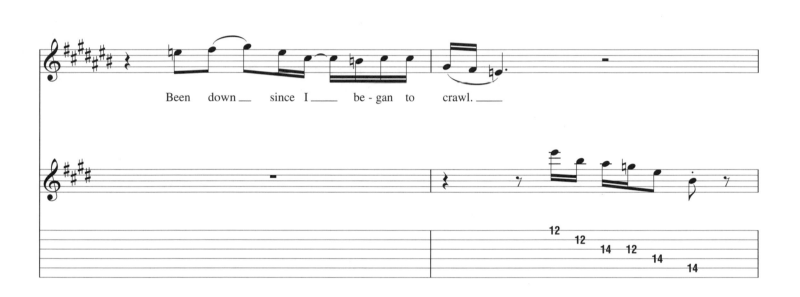

Been down _ since I __ be - gan to crawl. __

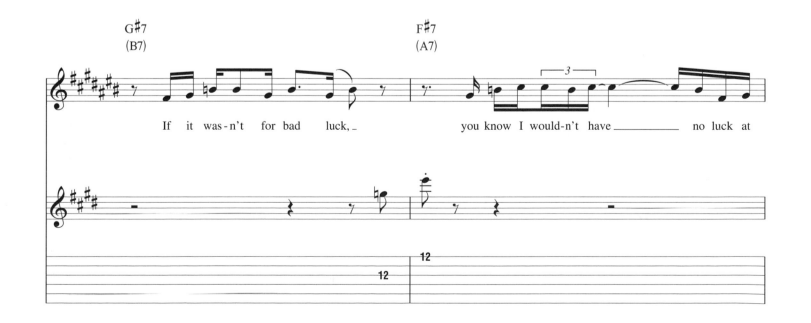

G#7
(B7)

F#7
(A7)

If it was - n't for bad luck, _ you know I would - n't have ___ no luck at

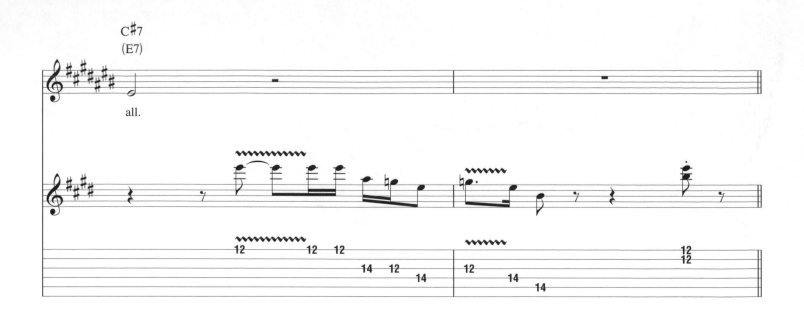

all.

Verse

Gtr. tacet

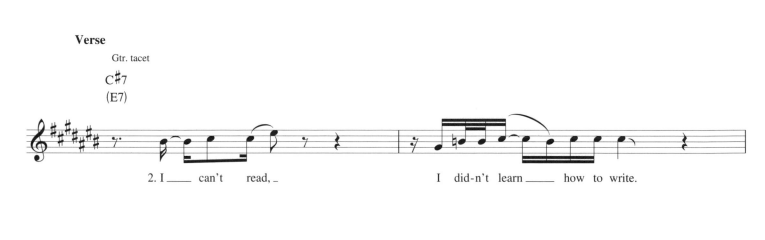

2. I ___ can't read, ___ I did-n't learn ___ how to write.

My whole ___ life ___ has been ___ one ___ big fight.

Chorus

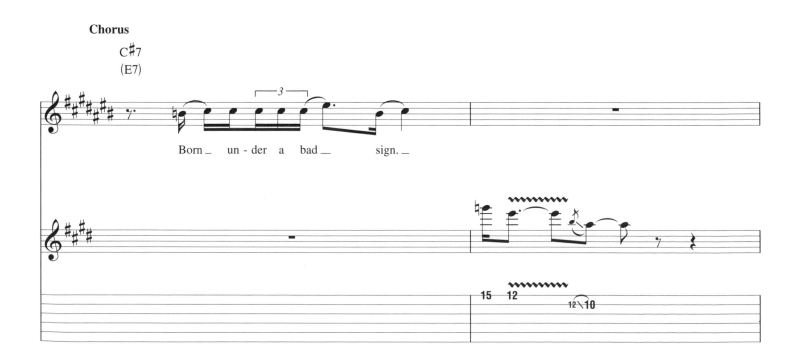

Born ___ un-der a bad ___ sign. ___

I been down___ since I___ be - gan to crawl.___

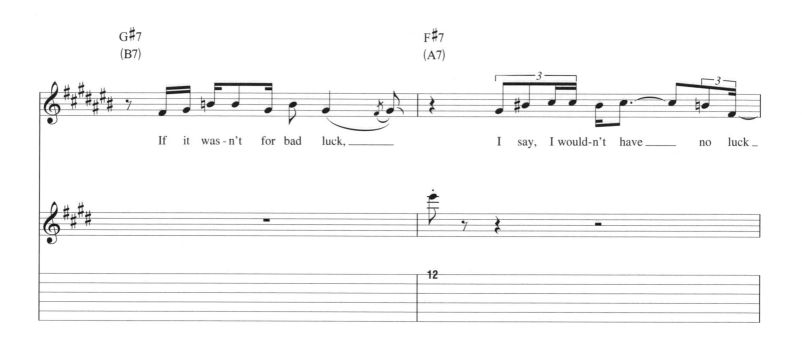

If it was-n't for bad luck,_____ I say, I would-n't have_____ no luck_

___ at all, *Spoken:* n' that ain't no lie. ___

Guitar Solo

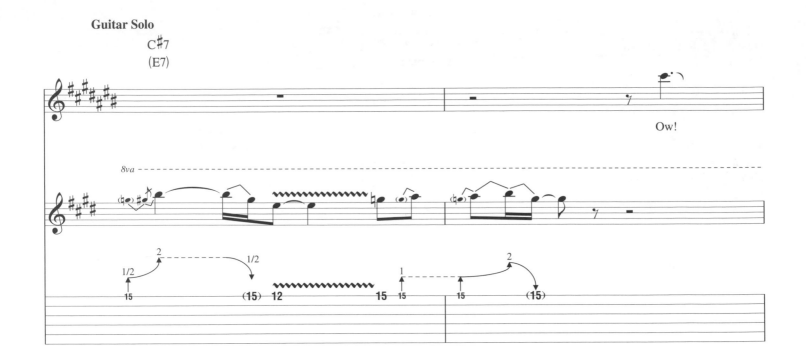

Ow!

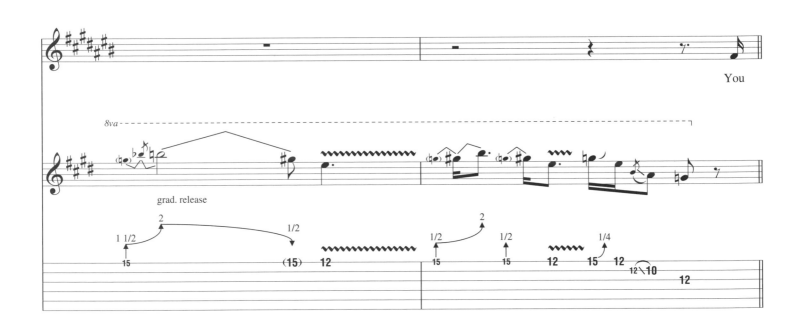

You

Bridge

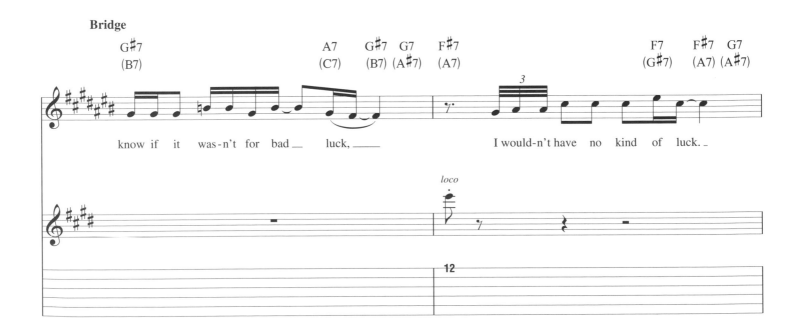

know if it was-n't for bad ___ luck, _____ I would-n't have no kind of luck. _

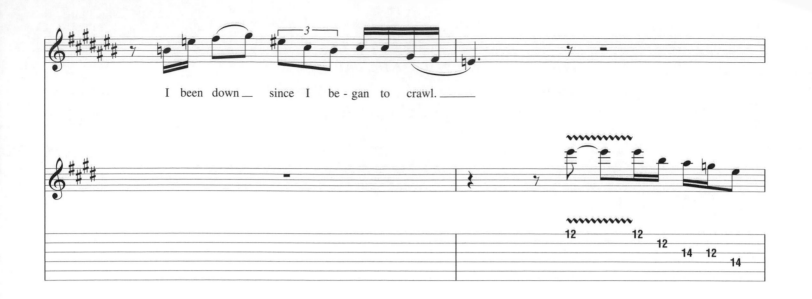

I been down— since I be-gan to crawl. ———

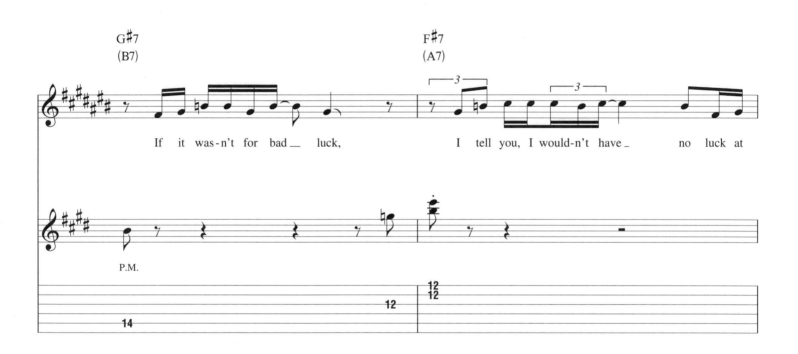

G#7
(B7)

F#7
(A7)

If it was-n't for bad— luck, I tell you, I would-n't have— no luck at

P.M.

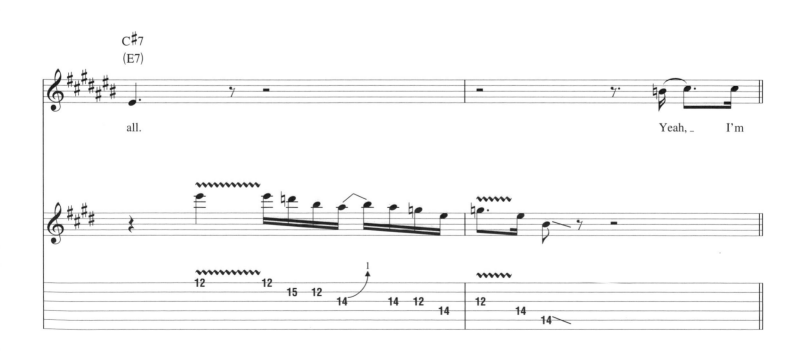

C#7
(E7)

all. Yeah,— I'm

Outro

C#7
(E7)

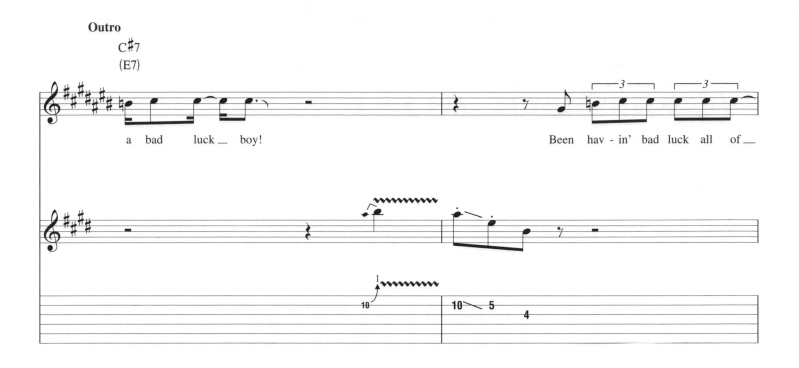

a bad luck __ boy!   Been hav - in' bad luck all of __

Begin fade

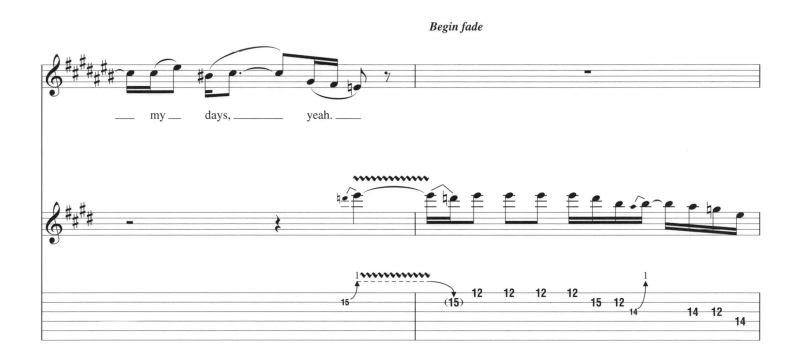

__ my __ days, _____ yeah. _____

Fade out

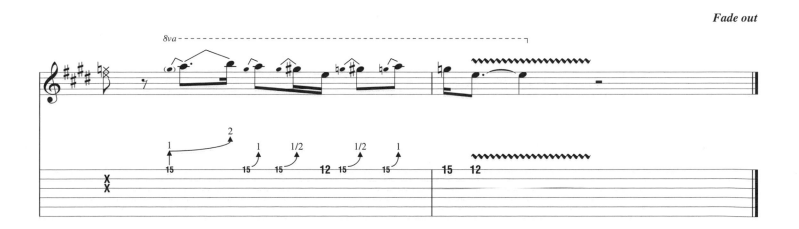

CROSS ROAD BLUES (CROSSROADS)
Cream

Video Lesson – 28 minutes, 29 seconds

Standard Tuning: (low to high) E–A–D–G–B–E
Key of A

Guitar Tone:

- medium distortion
- light reverb
- bridge pickup
- EQ: bass – 7, mid – 5, treble – 4

Scales:
Guitar Solos:

A Minor Pentatonic Hybrid Scale (5th pos.)

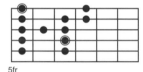

5fr

A Minor Pentatonic Hybrid Scale (17th pos.)

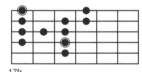

17fr

Techniques:

- Pull-Off/Hammer-On: the opening riff contains a compound slur, consisting of a pull-off/hammer-on/pull-off. Pull slightly down for the pull-off and land forcefully back on the string for the hammer-on. The same technique would apply for the other slurs found throughout the song.

- String Bending: as in most blues, string bending is a must-know technique. Be sure to keep your bend pitches in tune! Practice these by fretting the target pitches first to hear how far you should bend the strings to nail the proper pitches. Make sure you use some support fingers behind the fretted note.

- Vibrato: defined as a repeated fluctuation of pitch, vibrato is typically used on notes of a longer duration. It is achieved by bending and releasing a string over and over. Bent notes are also treated with vibrato. First, bend the note to the desired pitch, then subtly shake the string from this point (slightly bending above and/or below the position of the bent note).

- Palm Muting: rest the palm of your pick hand against the strings where they meet the bridge. The notes should sound muffled but still have pitch. If the notes don't have pitch, move your hand more towards the bridge. If the notes don't sound muffled, move your hand more towards the pickups.

- Unison Bend: keep the top note steady while you bend the lower note up to match its pitch.

- Double-Stop Bends: for the second Guitar Solo, grab the double-stop bends on the 19th fret with the ring finger, barring across to cover both strings.

Cross Road Blues
(Crossroads)

Words and Music by Robert Johnson

Intro
Moderately fast Rock ♩ = 130

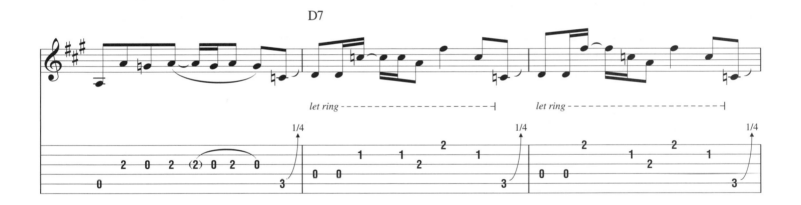

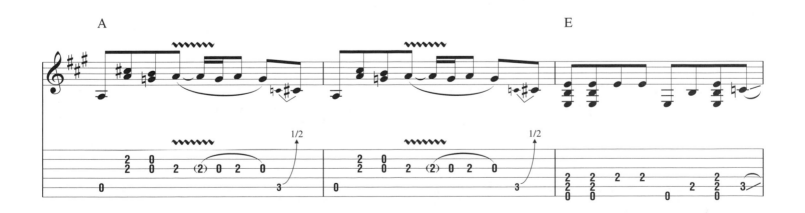

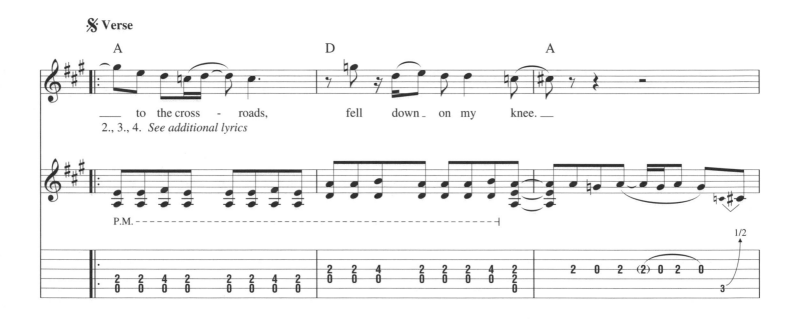

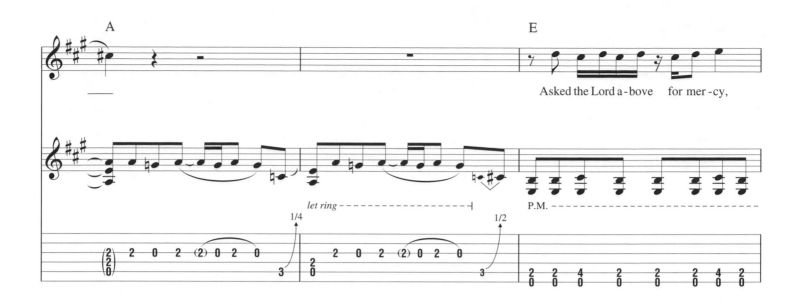

Asked the Lord a-bove   for mer -cy,

1., 2.

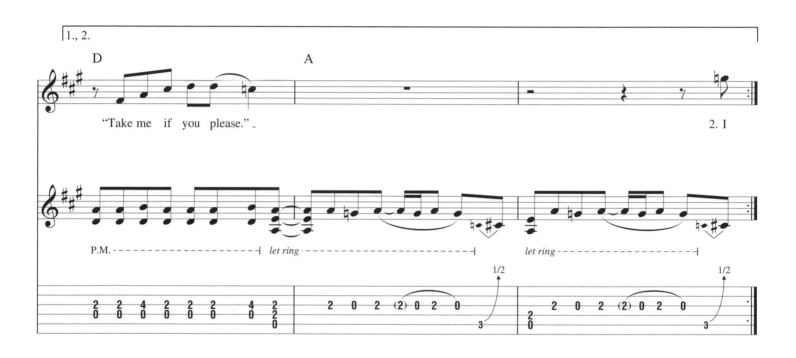

"Take me   if   you please." _

2. I

3.

To Coda

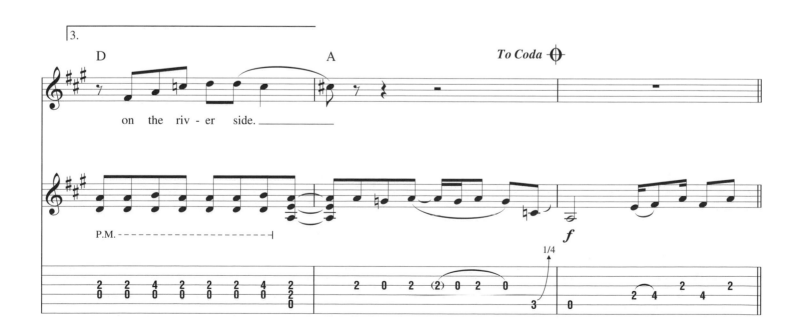

on   the   riv - er   side. _____

Guitar Solo

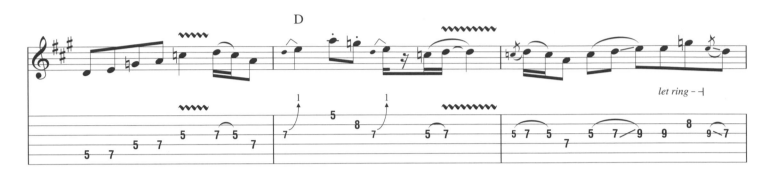

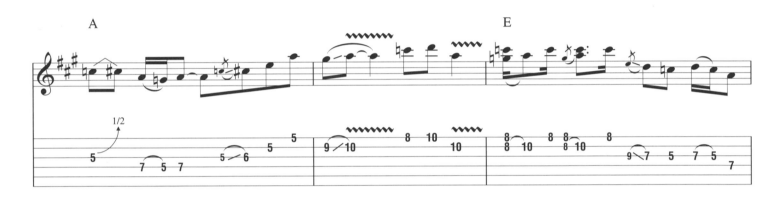

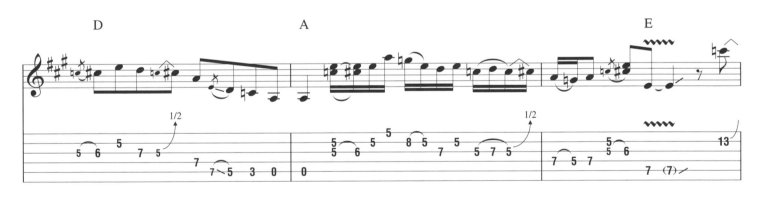

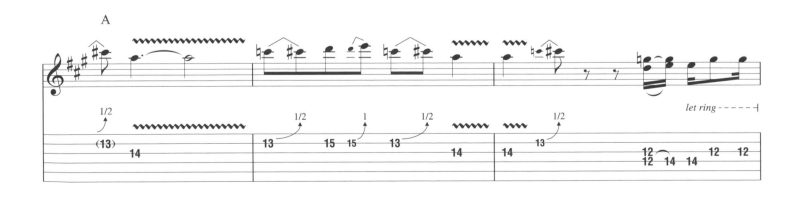

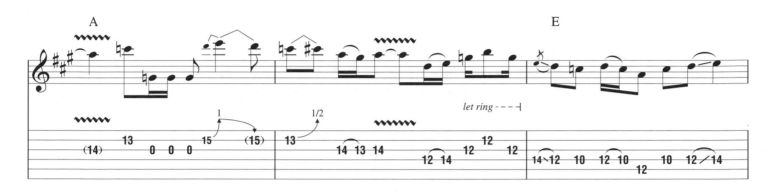

D.S. al Coda
(take 3rd ending)

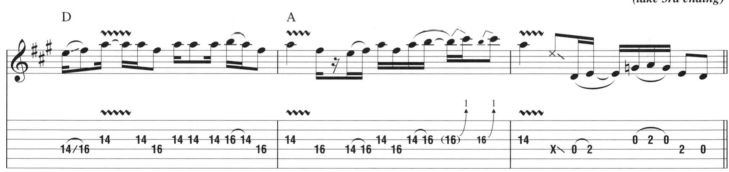

 Coda

Guitar Solo

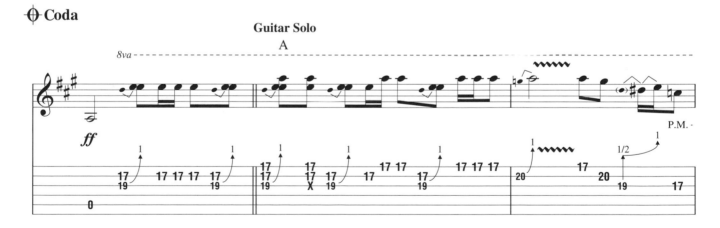

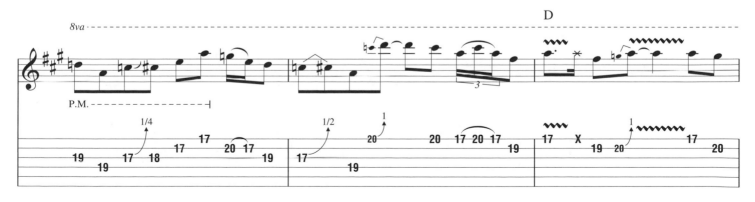

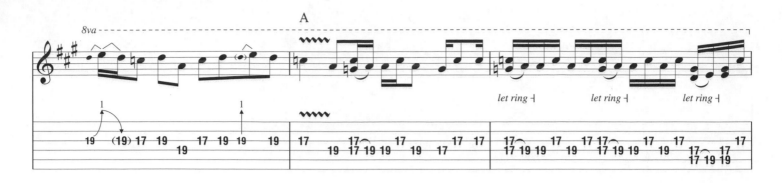

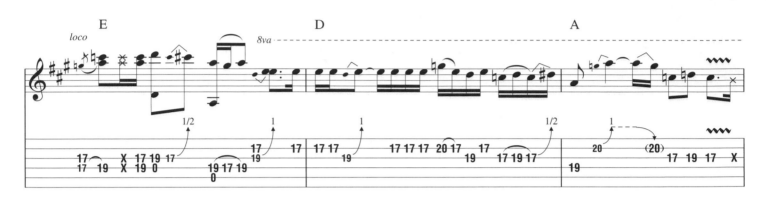

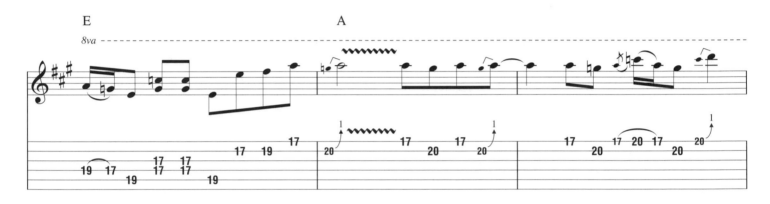

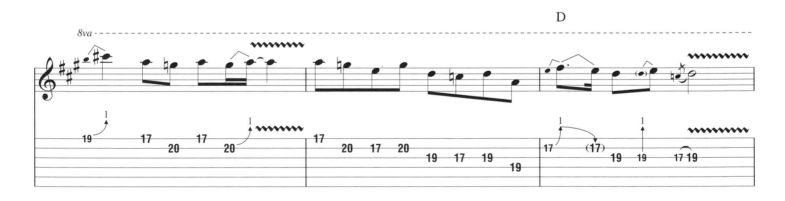

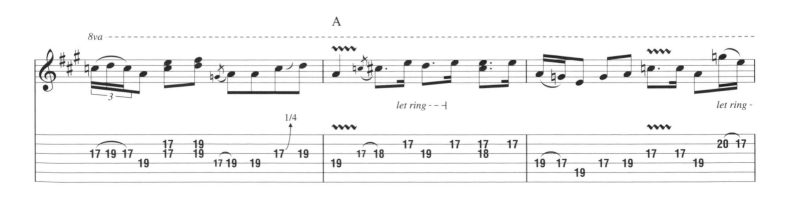

Outro-Verse

5. You can run, you can run, tell my friend, boy, Wil-lie Brown. ⎯

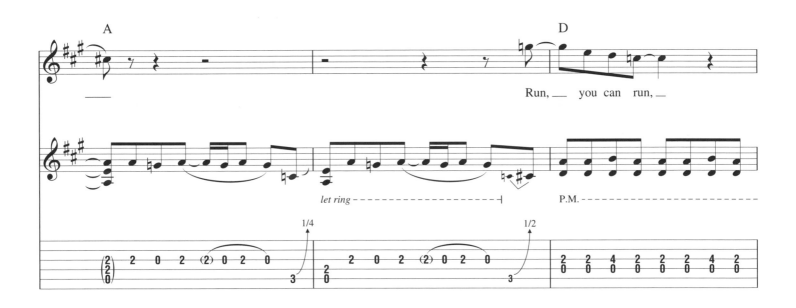

Run, ⎯ you can run, ⎯

tell my ⎯ friend, boy, Wil-lie Brown. ⎯ And I'm

stand-in' at the cross - road, be - lieve I'm __ sink - in' down.

P.M. ‑|

Free time

A7

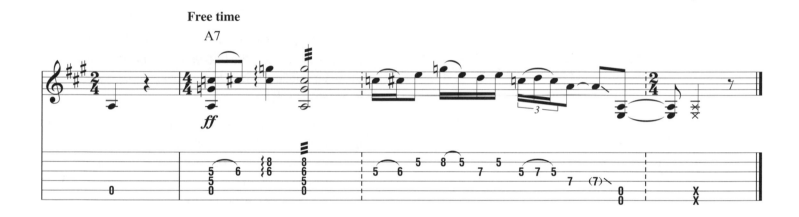

Additional Lyrics

2. I went down to the crossroad, tried to flag a ride.
   Down to the crossroad, tried to flag a ride.
   Nobody seemed to know me. Ev'rybody passed me by.

3., 4. When I'm goin' down to Rosedale, take my rider by my side.
   Goin' down to Rosedale, take my rider by my side.
   We can still barrelhouse, baby, on the riverside.

HIDE AWAY
Freddie King

Video Lesson – 23 minutes, 7 seconds

Standard Tuning: (low to high) E–A–D–G–B–E
Key of E

Guitar Tone:

- light distortion
- bridge pickup
- EQ: bass – 7, mid – 5, treble – 7

Chords:
Main Shuffle:

E6   E5   A5

A6   A7   B7

D Section:

B7

E Section:

E9

Techniques:

- Shuffle Feel vs. Straight Feel: the majority of the song is played with a shuffle feel (or swing feel). This means all 8th notes are playing in an uneven, long-short rhythm commonly heard in blues and jazz. However, the F section is played with a straight 8th feel, requiring regular, even 8th notes. Listen to the song to get a sense of these different rhythmic feels.

- Palm Muting: lightly rest the heel of your pick hand over the strings near the bridge while you are picking the main shuffle chords. Lift your palm off for the licks in between.

- Hammer-Ons: the melody of this tune includes a lot of hammer-ons. Focus on creating an even tone and volume for each hammered note and keep your fingers arched when you hammer down to the fretboard so you don't bump the adjacent strings.

- Trill: Section B starts with a trill, which is a rapid succession of alternating hammer-ons and pull-offs. Strive for a clean, clear trill and avoid bumping the other strings as you repeatedly hammer onto and pull off of the 2nd fret on the B string.

- Hybrid Picking: the dyads in Section E require the use of your pick and fingers. Pick the notes on the 3rd string with the pick while simultaneously plucking the 1st-string notes with your middle finger.

Dyads:
Section E:

E Major/Minor Pentatonic Dyads

Hide Away

By Freddie King and Sonny Thompson

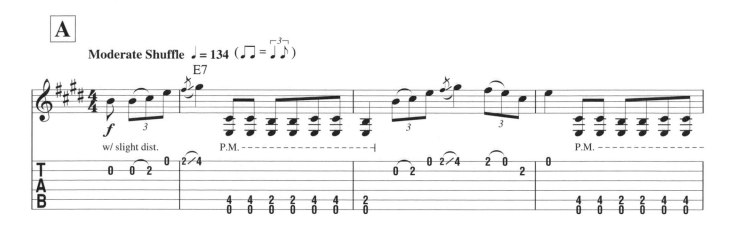

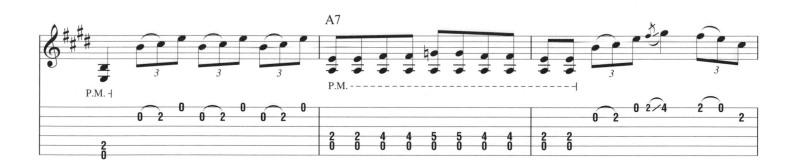

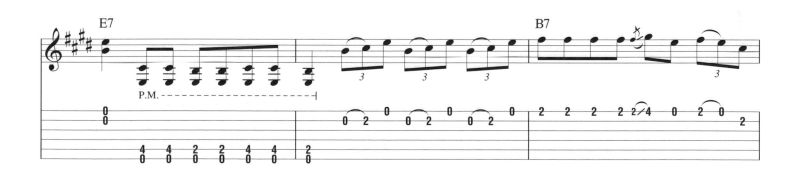

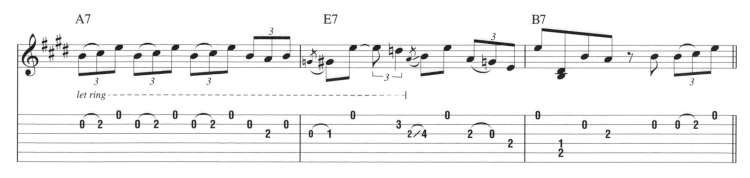

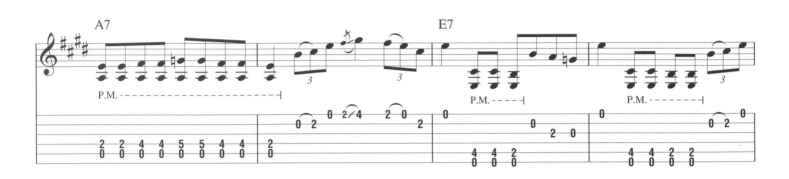

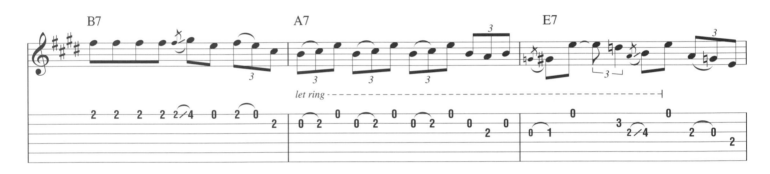

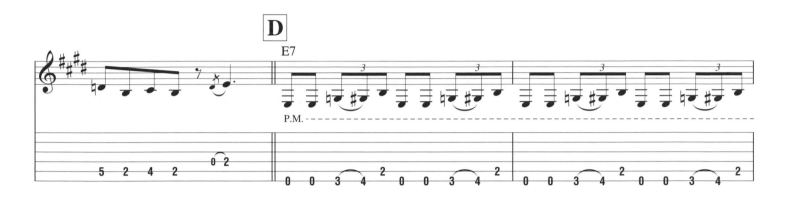

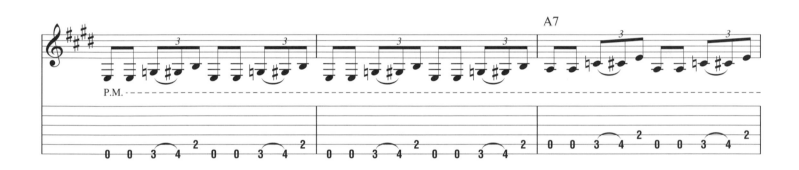

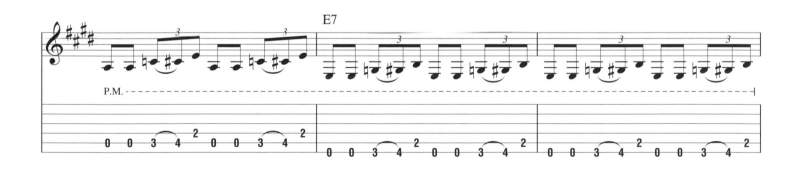

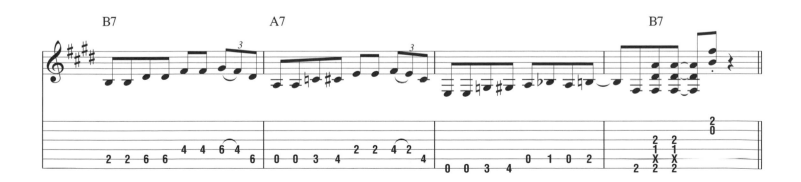

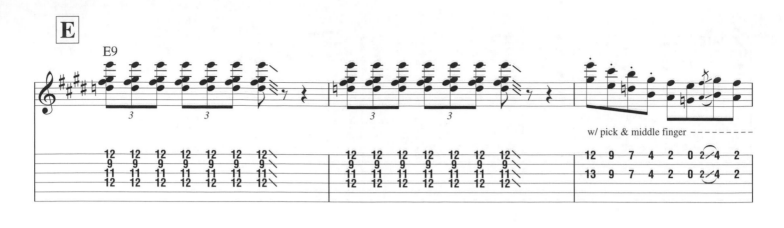

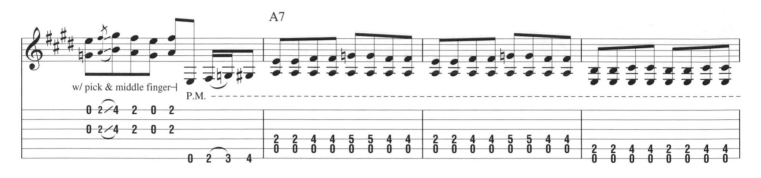

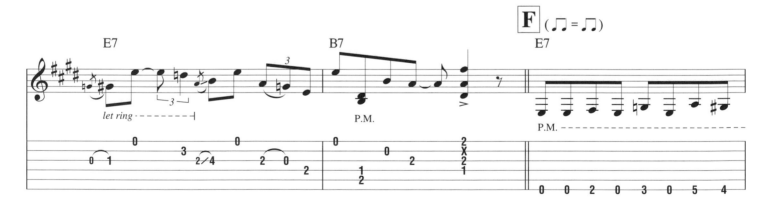

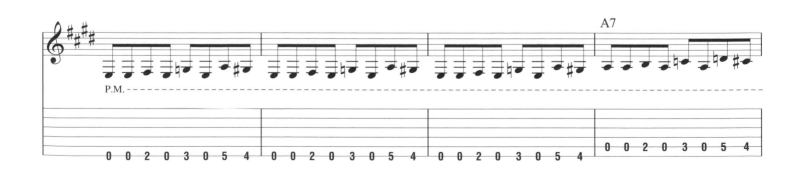

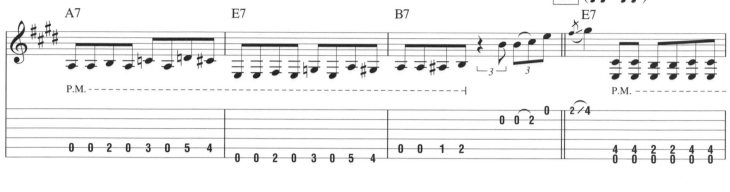

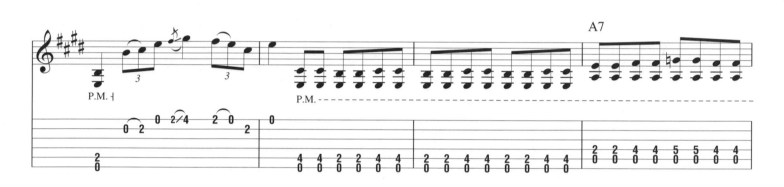

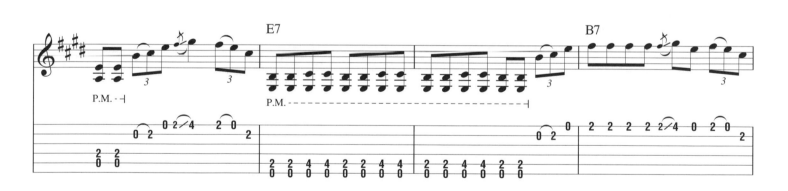

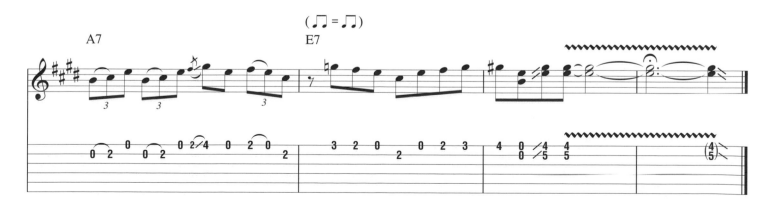

I'M TORE DOWN
Eric Clapton

Video Lesson – 17 minutes, 13 seconds

Standard Tuning: (low to high) E–A–D–G–B–E
Key of C

Guitar Tone:

- medium distortion
- light reverb
- bridge pickup
- EQ: bass – 6, mid – 5, treble – 5

Chords:
Verse 1:

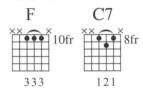

Verse 2:

Outro-Chorus:

Techniques:

- String Bending: as in most blues, string bending is a must-know technique. Be sure to keep your bend pitches in tune! Practice these by fretting the target pitches first to hear how far you should bend the strings to nail the proper pitches. Make sure you use some support fingers behind the fretted note.

- Vibrato: defined as a repeated fluctuation of pitch, vibrato is typically used on notes of a longer duration. It is achieved by bending and releasing a string over and over. Bent notes are also treated with vibrato. First, bend the note to the desired pitch, then subtly shake the string from this point (slightly bending above and/ or below the position of the bent note).

- Staccato: notes or chords with a dot over them indicate staccato. This means they should be cut short and not allowed to ring out. After the initial attack, use your left and right hands to mute the strings.

Scales:

C Minor Pentatonic Hybrid Scale

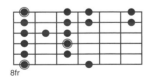

I'm Tore Down

Words and Music by Sonny Thompson

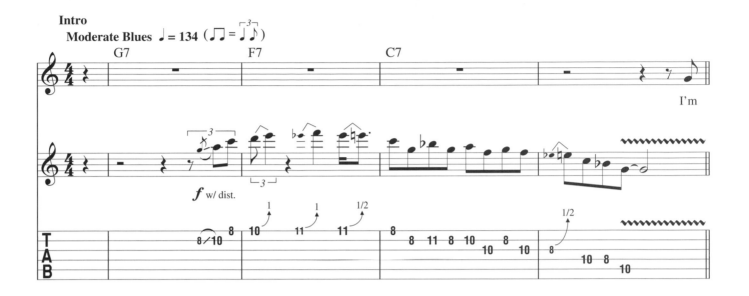

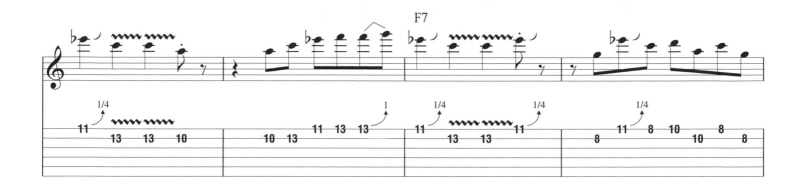

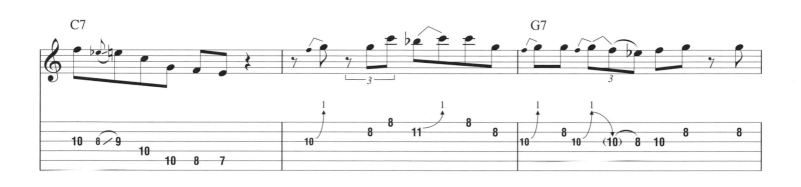

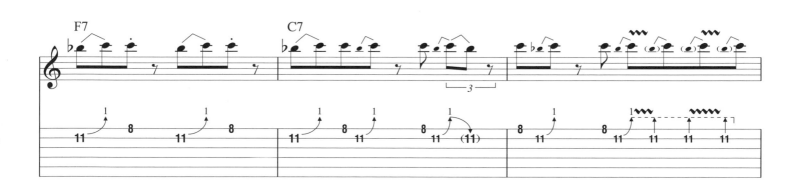

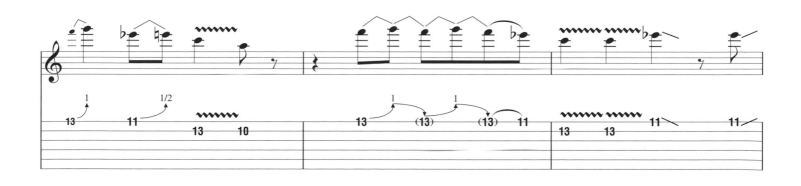

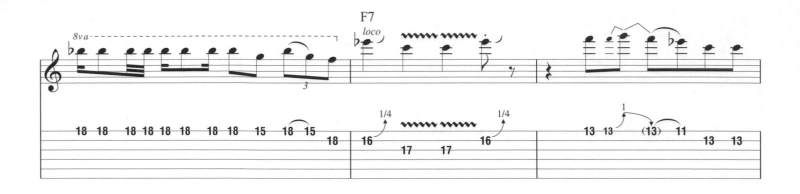

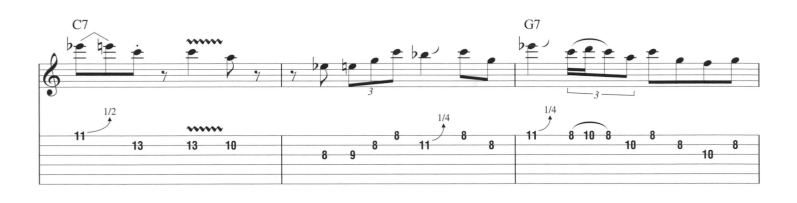

D.S. al Coda

Additional Lyrics

3. Love you, baby, with all my might.
   Love like mine is outta sight.
   I'll lie for you if you want me to.
   I really don't believe that your love is true.

I'M YOUR HOOCHIE COOCHIE MAN
Muddy Waters

Video Lesson – 14 minutes, 44 seconds

Standard Tuning: (low to high) E–A–D–G–B–E
Key of A

Guitar Tone:

- light distortion
- light reverb
- bridge pickup
- EQ: bass – 6, mid – 4, treble – 6

Scales/Arpeggios:
Chorus:

D7 Arpeggio

A7 Arpeggio

E7 Arpeggio

2fr

Guitar Solo:

A Blues Hybrid Scale

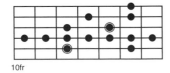

10fr

Techniques:

- String Bending: as in most blues, string bending is a must-know technique. Be sure to keep your bend pitches in tune! Practice these by fretting the target pitches first to hear how far you should bend the strings to nail the proper pitches. Make sure you use some support fingers behind the fretted note.

- Vibrato: defined as a repeated fluctuation of pitch, vibrato is typically used on notes of a longer duration. It is achieved by bending and releasing a string over and over. Bent notes are also treated with vibrato. First, bend the note to the desired pitch, then subtly shake the string from this point (slightly bending above and/or below the position of the bent note).

- Staccato: notes or chords with a dot over them indicate staccato. This means they should be cut short and not allowed to ring out. After the initial attack, use your left and right hands to mute the strings.

I'm Your Hoochie Coochie Man

Words and Music by Willie Dixon

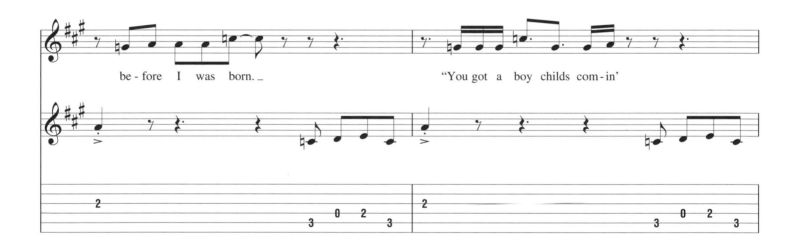

jump an' shout. __   Then the world wan-na know

Chorus
D7

what this all a - bout?" __   But you know I'm here. ___

A7

Ev - 'ry - bod - y knows __ I'm here. ___

To Coda ⊕
E7

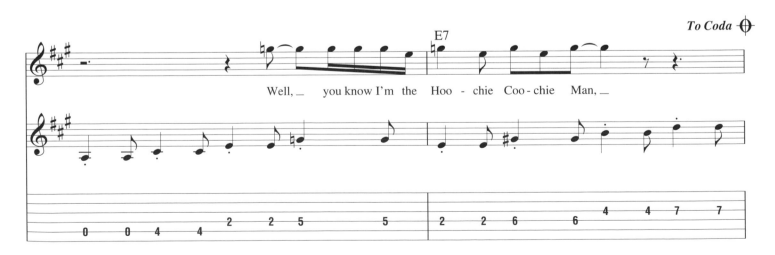

Well, __ you know I'm the Hoo - chie Coo - chie Man, __

ev - 'ry - bod - y   knows I'm   here. ___

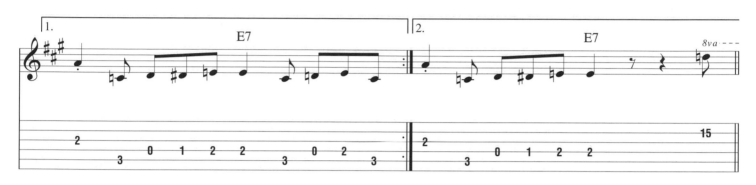

Guitar Solo

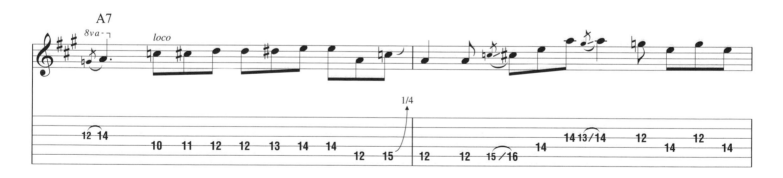

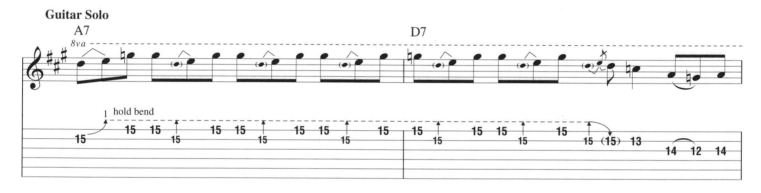

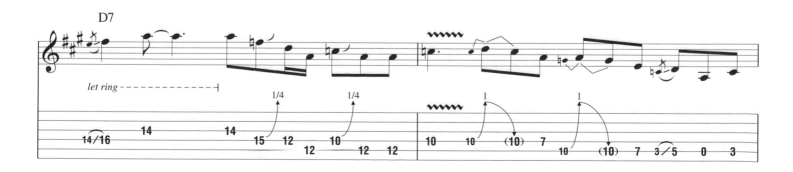

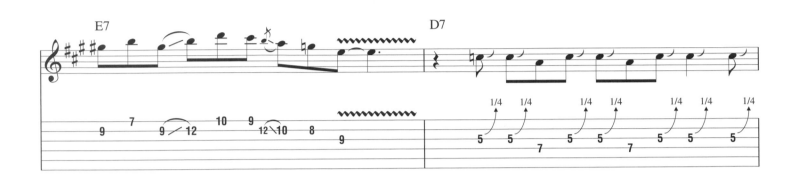

D.S. al Coda

the whole _ round world knows I'm here.

Additional Lyrics

2. I got a black cat bone,
   I got a mojo too.
   I got the John the Conquerroot,
   I'm gonna mess with you.
   I'm gonna make you girls
   Lead me by my hand.
   Then the world'll know
   I'm the Hoochie Coochie man.

3. On the seventh hour,
   On the seventh day,
   On the seventh month,
   The seventh doctor say,
   "You were born for good luck,
   And that you'll see."
   I got seven hundred dollars,
   Don't you mess with me.

KILLING FLOOR
Howlin' Wolf

Video Lesson – 13 minutes, 38 seconds

Standard Tuning: (low to high) E–A–D–G–B–E
Key of A

Guitar Tone:

- medium distortion
- light reverb
- bridge pickup
- EQ: bass – 4, mid – 5, treble – 6

Chords:

Intro:

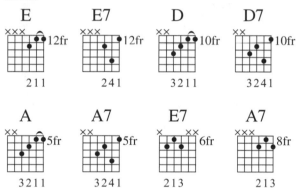

Techniques:

- 6th Intervals: use your 2nd and 3rd fingers to fret these intervals on the 3rd and 1st strings, allowing your 2nd finger to lightly touch the 2nd string, muting it. Strum through all three strings, making sure that the 2nd string is muted and not producing a pitch.

- Upward Slides: some notes and chords finish with an upward slide. After plucking the note or chord, quickly slide up the neck.

- Chord Riffs: the song is built around various chord-type riffs. Get to know the different shapes and versions for each chord. It's very beneficial to know multiple voicings for the same chord.

Killing Floor

Words and Music by Chester Burnett

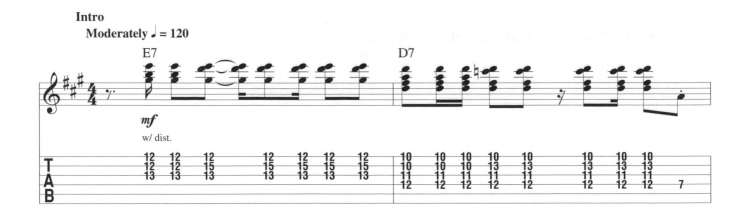

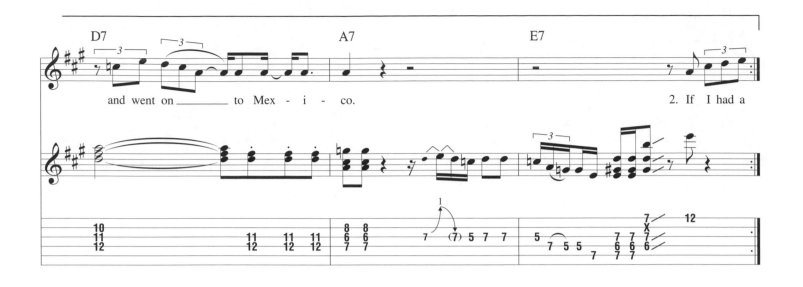

and went on ____ to Mex - i - co.   2. If I had a

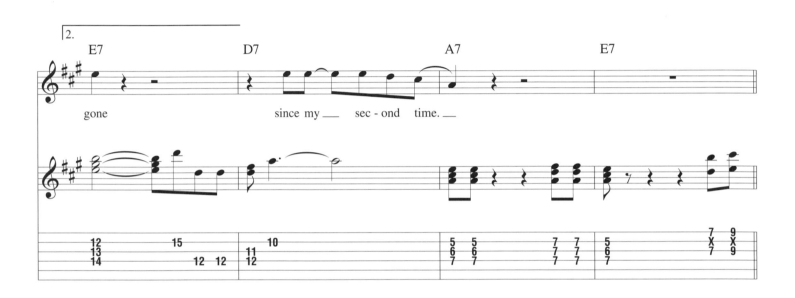

gone   since my ___ sec - ond   time. ___

Guitar Solo

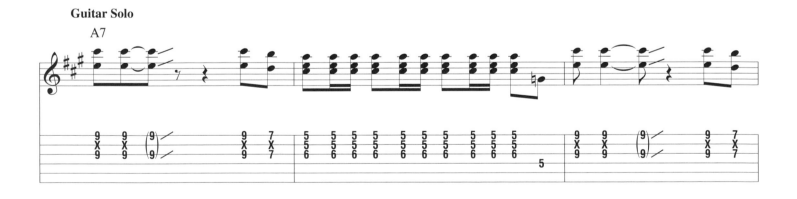

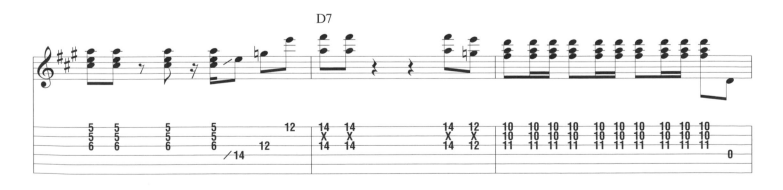

D.S. al Coda 1

3. I should have

⊕ Coda 1

fool - in' with you, ba - by, I let you put me on the ___ kill - ing

D.S. al Coda 2

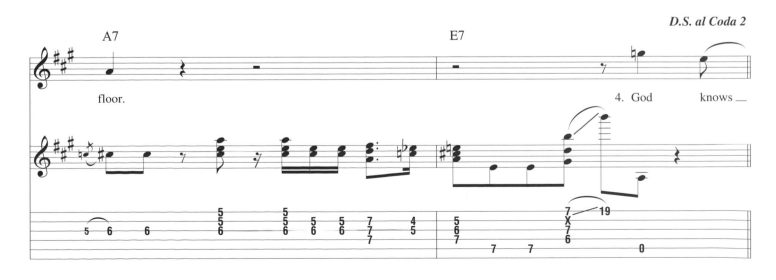

floor.

4. God knows ___

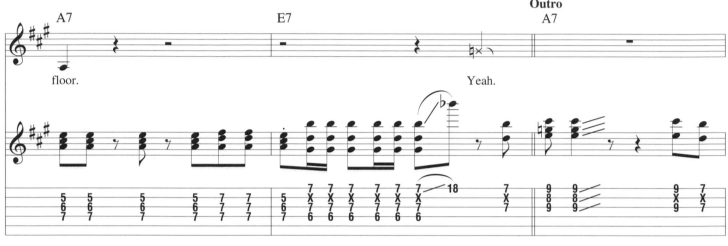

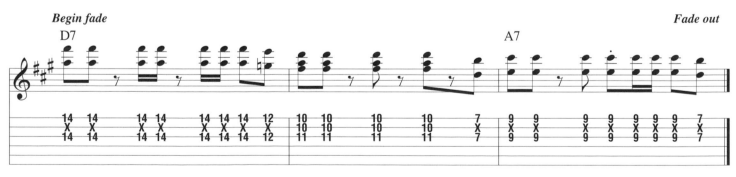

Additional Lyrics

2. If I had a followed my first mind,
   If I had a followed my first mind,
   I'd a been gone since my second time.

3. I should have went on when my friend come from Mexico at me.
   I should have went on when my friend come from Mexico at me.
   But now I'm foolin' with you, baby, I let you put me on the killing floor.

4. God knows I should have been gone.
   God knows I should have been gone.
   Then I wouldn't have been here, down on the killing floor.

MARY HAD A LITTLE LAMB
Buddy Guy

Video Lesson – 17 minutes, 32 seconds

Standard Tuning: (low to high) E–A–D–G–B–E
Key of E

Guitar Tone:

- clean tone

- light reverb

- neck pickup

- EQ: bass – 5, mid – 5, treble – 7

Chords:

Intro:

Scales:

E Minor Pentatonic Scale

12fr

Techniques:

- String Bending: as in most blues, string bending is a must-know technique. Be sure to keep your bend pitches in tune! Practice these by fretting the target pitches first to hear how far you should bend the strings to nail the proper pitches. Make sure you use some support fingers behind the fretted note.

- Double Stops: for the double stops in the Guitar Solo on frets 17 and 15, use a barred 3rd and 1st finger, respectively.

- Vibrato: defined as a repeated fluctuation of pitch, vibrato is typically used on notes of a longer duration. It is achieved by bending and releasing a string over and over. Bent notes are also treated with vibrato. First, bend the note to the desired pitch, then subtly shake the string from this point (slightly bending above and/ or below the position of the bent note).

Mary Had a Little Lamb

Words and Music by Buddy Guy

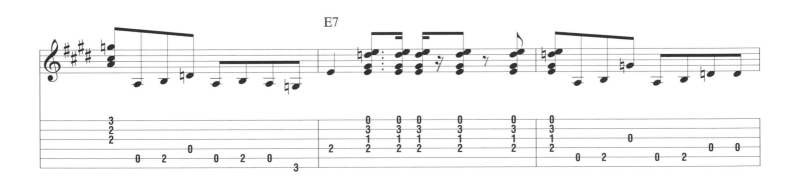

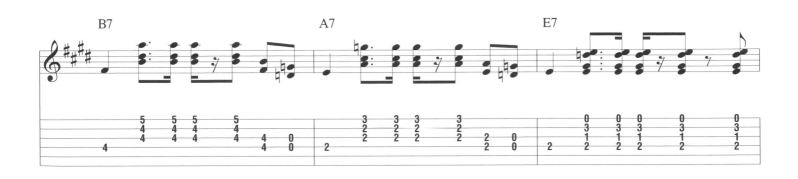

Verse

N.C.　　　　　　　　A7

1. Mar-y had a lit-tle lamb, _____　　　its fleece was white as snow,

2. *See additional lyrics*

E7　　　　　　　　　　　　　　　　　　B7

yeah. __　　　Ev-'ry-where the child　went,

A7　　　　　　　　　　　　　　　　　　E7

the lamb, __　the lamb was sure to　go, yeah.

1.

2. He fol-lowed her to school __ Uh.

2.　　　　　　**Guitar Solo**

A7

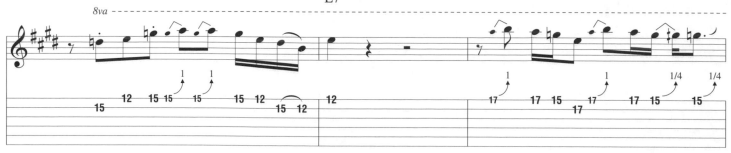

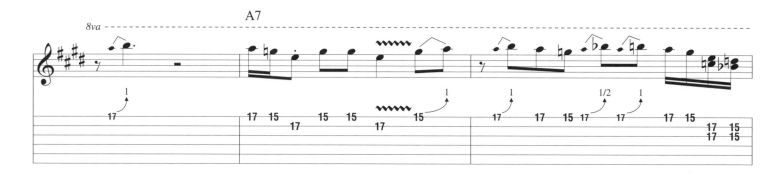

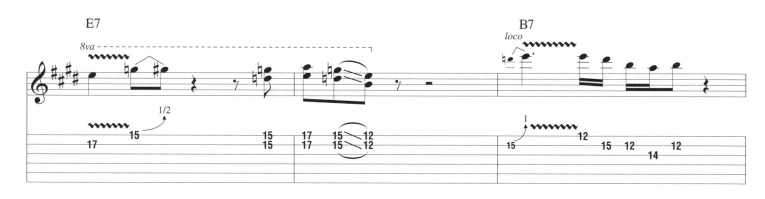

3. Tis - ket,

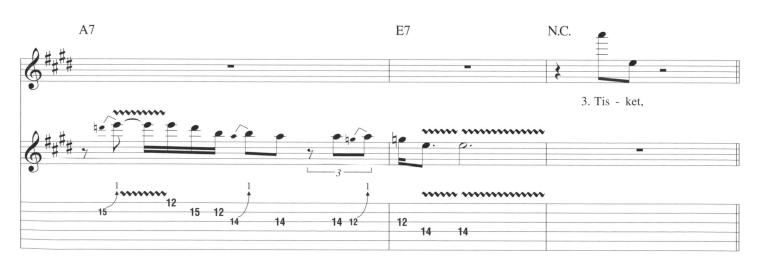

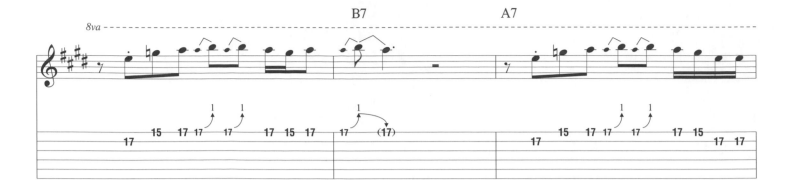

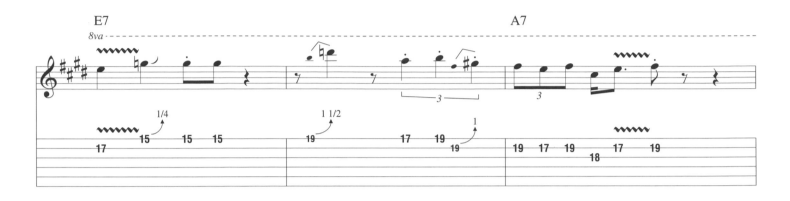

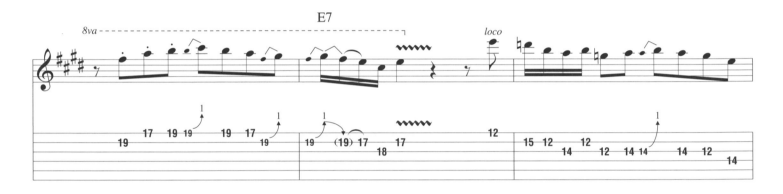

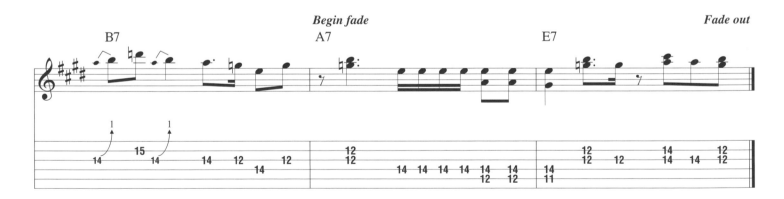

Additional Lyrics

2. He followed her to school one day
   And broke the teacher's rule.
   And what a time did they have
   That day at school.

4. No, no, no, no, no, no, oo.
   No, no, no, no, yeah.
   No, no, no, no, no, yeah.
   No, no, no, no, no, no, yeah.
   Uh, uh, uh, uh. Hit it.

STILL GOT THE BLUES
Gary Moore

Video Lesson – 21 minutes, 51 seconds

Standard Tuning: (low to high) E–A–D–G–B–E
Key of A minor

Guitar Tone:

- heavy distortion

- neck pickup and bridge pickup (Outro-Guitar Solo)

- EQ: bass – 5, mid – 6, treble – 8

Chords:
Chorus:

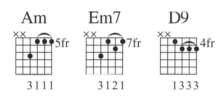

Am   Em7   D9
3 1 1 1   3 1 2 1   1 3 3 3

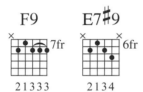

F9   E7#9
2 1 3 3 3   2 1 3 4

Bridge:

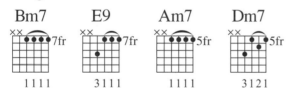

Bm7   E9   Am7   Dm7
1 1 1 1   3 1 1 1   1 1 1 1   3 1 2 1

Arpeggios/Scales:
Verse:

Dm7 Arpeggio

Dm7/G Arpeggio

Cmaj7 Arpeggio

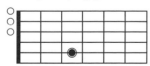

Fmaj7 Arpeggio

Bm7♭5 Arpeggio

E7 Arpeggio

Am Arpeggio

Guitar Solos:

A Minor Pentatonic Scale 1

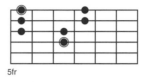

5fr

A Minor Pentatonic Scale 2

7fr

A Minor Pentatonic Scale 3

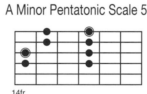

9fr

A Minor Pentatonic Scale 4

12fr

A Minor Pentatonic Scale 5

14fr

Techniques:

- String Bending: as in most blues, string bending is a must-know technique. Be sure to keep your bend pitches in tune! Practice these by fretting the target pitches first to hear how far you should bend the strings to nail the proper pitches. Make sure you use some support fingers behind the fretted note.

- Vibrato: defined as a repeated fluctuation of pitch, vibrato is typically used on notes of a longer duration. It is achieved by bending and releasing a string over and over. For this song, strive for a smooth, relatively slow vibrato. Bent notes are also treated with vibrato. First, bend the note to the desired pitch, then subtly shake the string from this point (slightly bending above and/ or below the position of the bent note).

- Rake: the main theme of this song contains rakes. With a specific target note in mind, quickly sweep the pick across the lower, adjacent strings until you reach the target note. The non-target notes are muted with the fret hand, adding more weight to the final destination note.

- Staccato: notes or chords with a dot over them indicate staccato. This means they should be cut short and not allowed to ring out. After the initial attack, use your left and right hands to mute the strings.

Still Got the Blues

Words and Music by Gary Moore

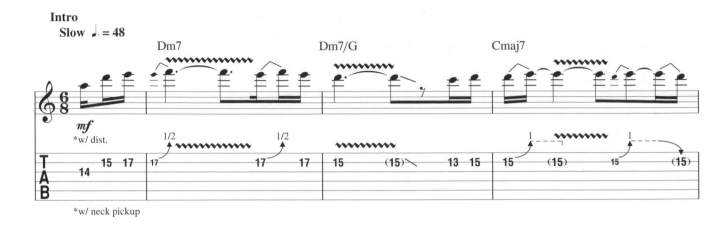

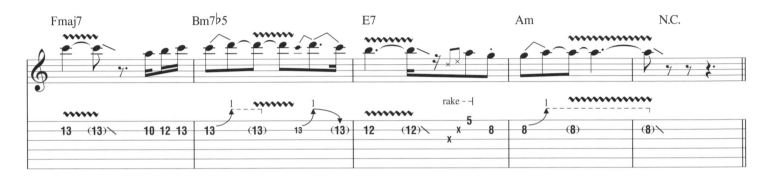

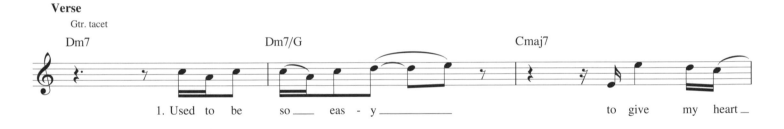

Verse

Gtr. tacet

1. Used to be so ___ eas-y ___ to give my heart ___

___ a-way, ___ but I found out the hard ___ way ___ there's a

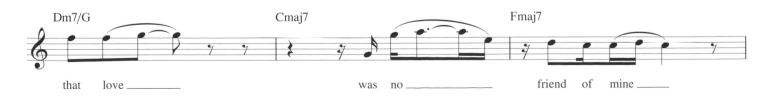

price ___ you have ___ to pay. ___ I ___ found out

that love ___ was no ___ friend of mine ___

but I found out the ___ hard ___ way   it's a   road _____ that leads

to   pain. ___   Well, I   found ___ that love _____

was   more _____ than ___ just a   game, ___   you're play - in'

to   win _____   but you'll   lose _____ just _____ the   same. _____

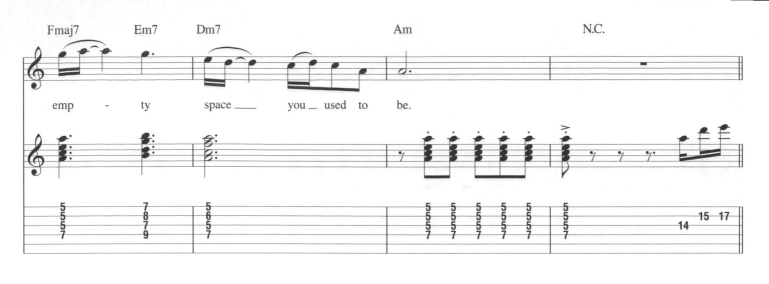

emp - ty space ___ you ___ used to be.

Guitar Solo

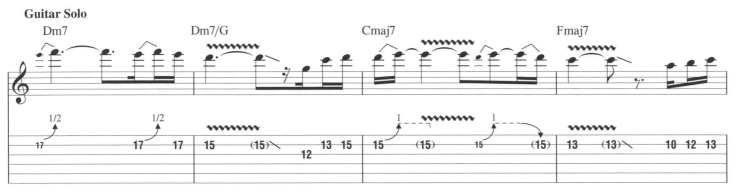

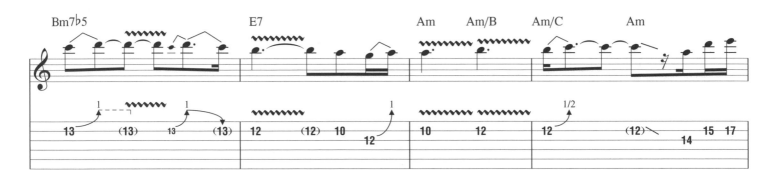

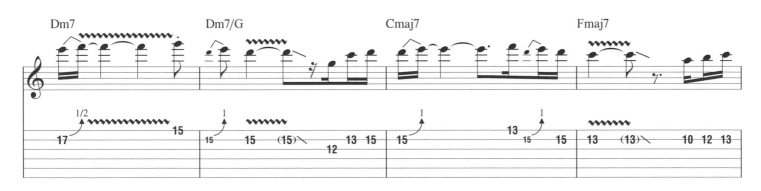

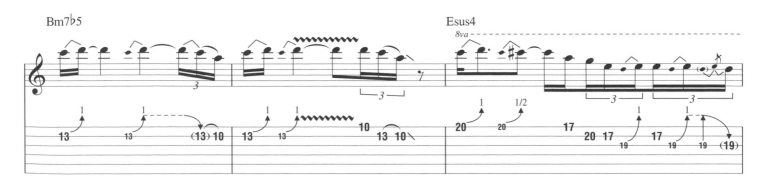

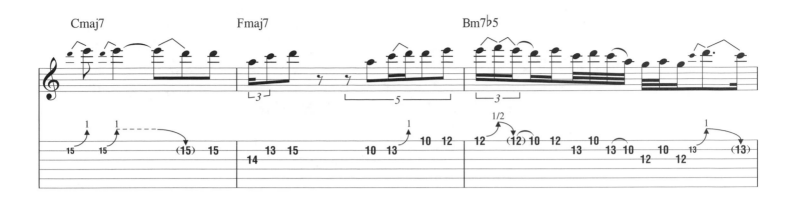

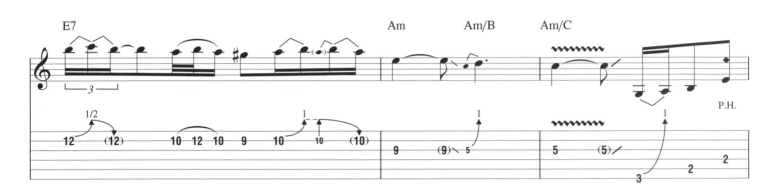

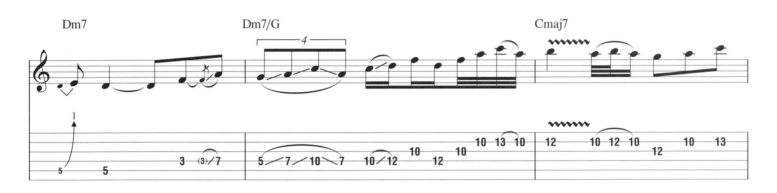

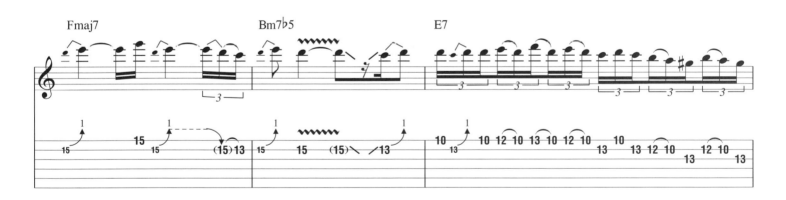

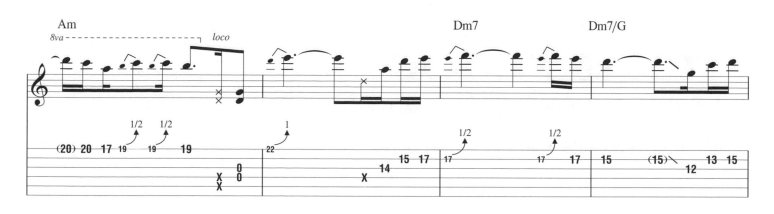

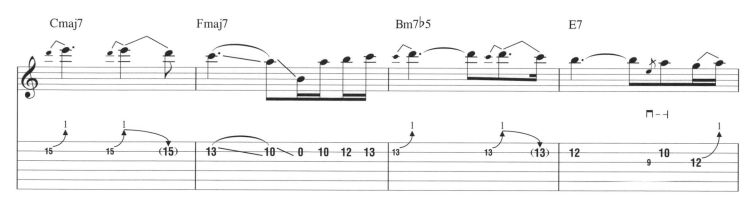

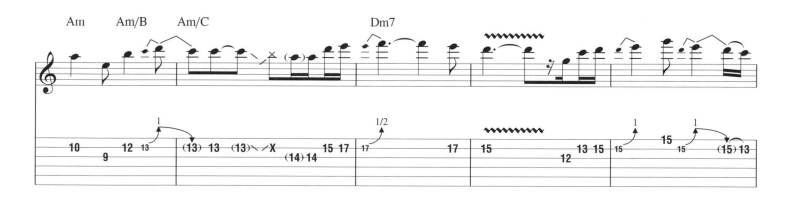

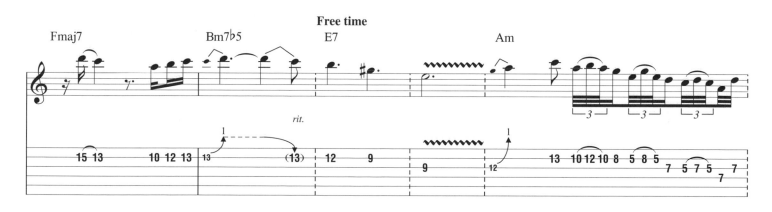

TEXAS FLOOD
Stevie Ray Vaughan and Double Trouble

Video Lesson – 29 minutes, 32 seconds

Tune Down 1/2 Step: (low to high) Eb–Ab–Db–Gb–Bb–Eb
Key of G

Guitar Tone:

- light distortion
- light reverb
- neck pickup
- EQ: bass – 8, mid – 5, treble – 7

Chords:
Verse 3:

D9

1 3 3 3

Db9

1 3 3 3

C9

1 3 3 3

G9

9fr
2 1 3 3 3
(4 4 4)

G9

1 2 1 3 4

Scales:

G Minor Pentatonic Hybrid Scale

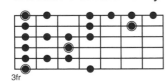
3fr

Techniques:

- String Bending: as in most blues, string bending is a must-know technique. Be sure to keep your bend pitches in tune! Practice these by fretting the target pitches first to hear how far you should bend the strings to nail the proper pitches. Make sure you use some support fingers behind the fretted note.

- Vibrato: defined as a repeated fluctuation of pitch, vibrato is typically used on notes of a longer duration. It is achieved by bending and releasing a string over and over. Bent notes are also treated with vibrato. First, bend the note to the desired pitch, then subtly shake the string from this point (slightly bending above and/ or below the position of the bent note).

- Hammer-Ons/Pull-Offs: for hammer-ons, strike the first note and then come down forcefully with your fret-hand finger to sound the next note. For the pull-off, strike the first note while also fretting the second note below it. Pull off in a slightly downward motion, allowing the second note to ring. Be careful not to sound the higher string with your pull-off finger.

- Rake: drag your pick across the indicated strings with one continuous motion while muting them with your fret hand.

- Double-Stop Bends: grab both strings with one finger in a barre technique. Keeping pressure down on the fingerboard, push the notes up to achieve the bend.

Texas Flood

Words and Music by Larry Davis and Joseph W. Scott

Tune down 1/2 step:
(low to high) Eb-Ab-Db-Gb-Bb-Eb

Intro
Slow Blues ♩ = 60

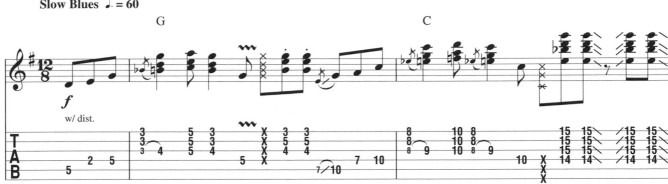

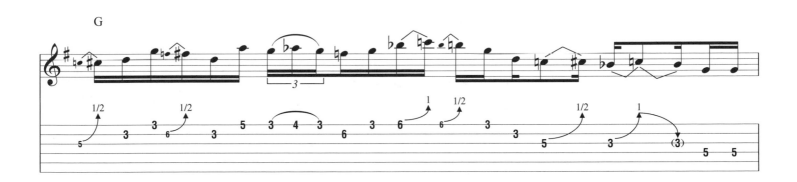

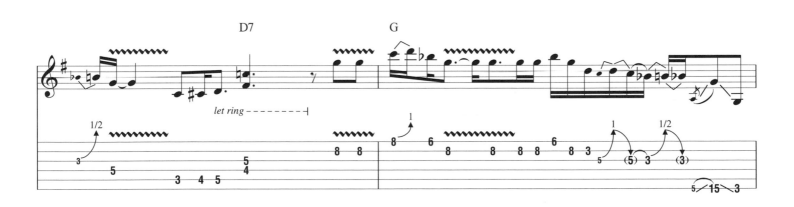

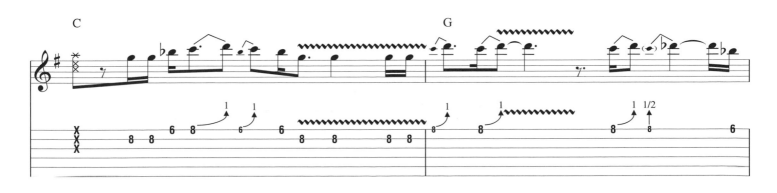

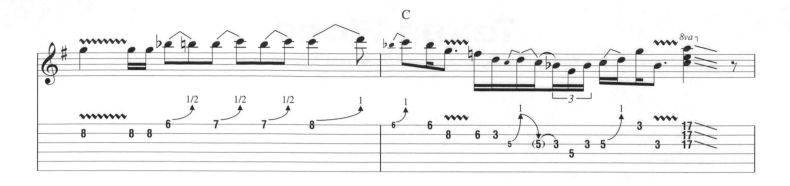

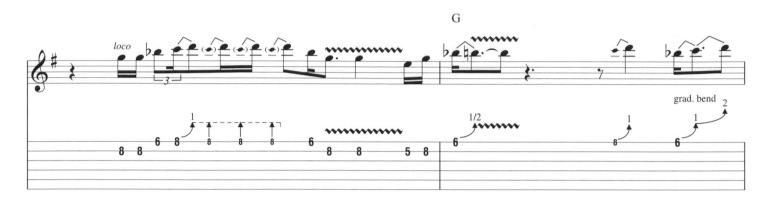

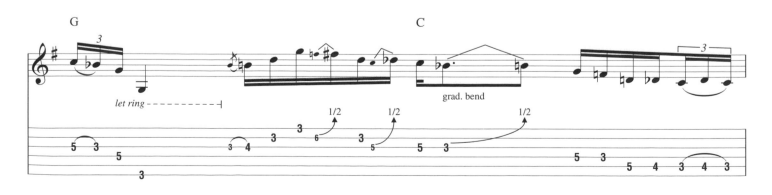

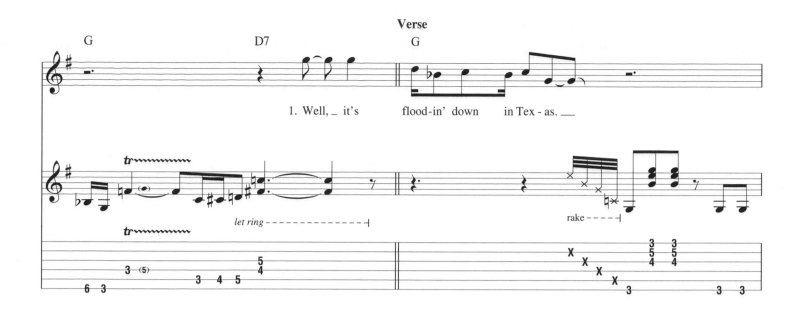

1. Well, __ it's flood-in' down in Tex - as. __

All of the tel - e-phone lines __ are down. __

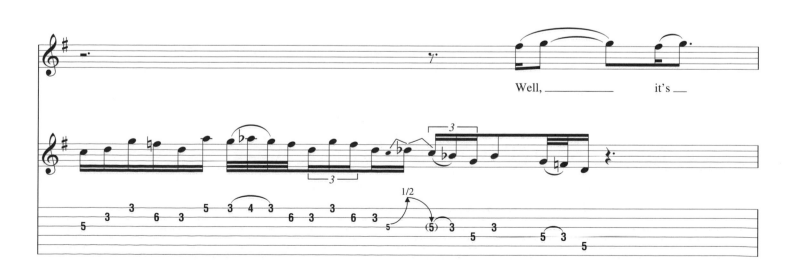

Well, _____ it's __

flood-in' down ___ in Tex-as. ___   All ___ of the tel-e-phone lines ___ are down. _

Yeah, ___ I been

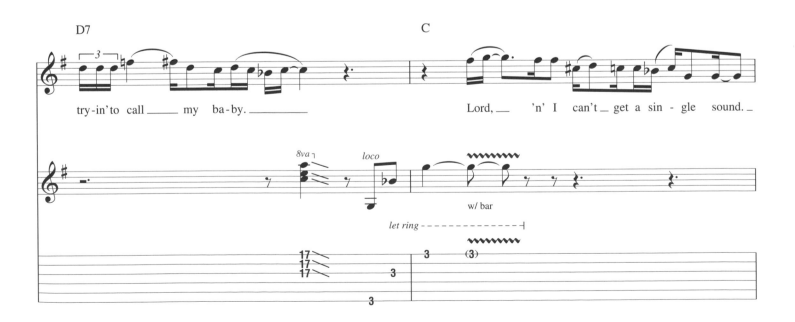

try-in'to call ___ my ba-by. ___   Lord, ___ 'n' I can't _ get a sin - gle   sound. _

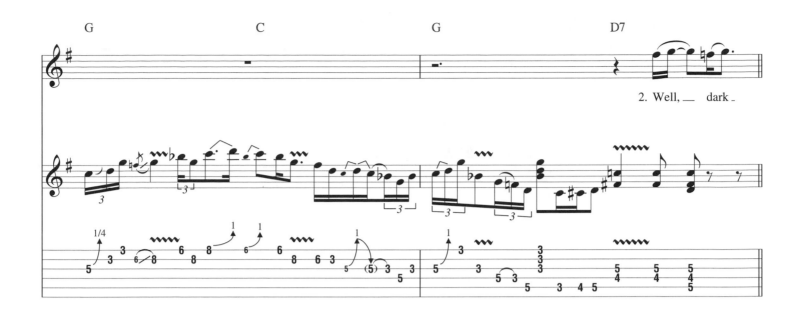

2. Well, ___ dark _

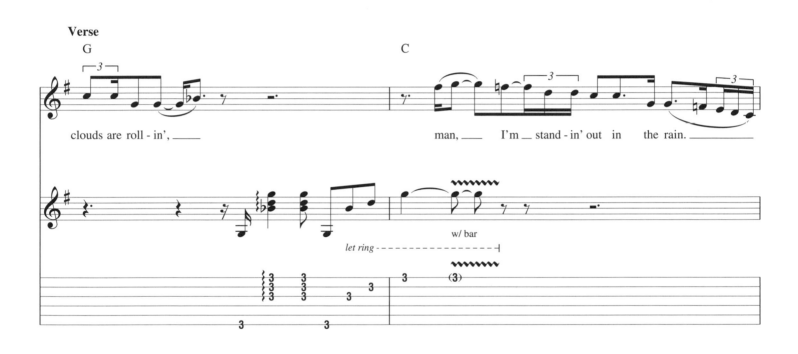

Verse

clouds are roll - in', _____ man, ___ I'm _ stand - in' out in the rain. _____

let ring - - - - - - - - - - - - - - - - - - -|

w/ bar

Well, _____ dark _

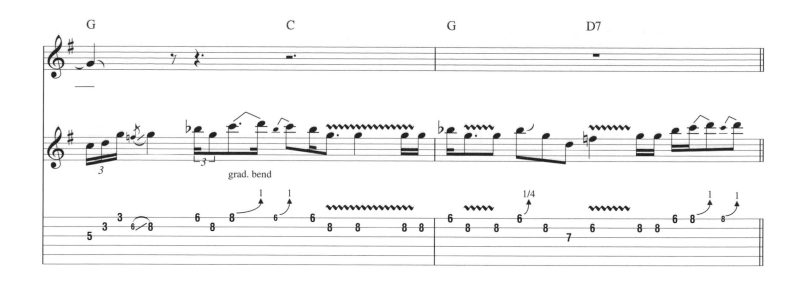

Guitar Solo

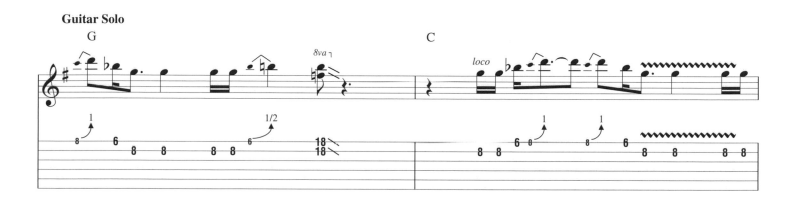

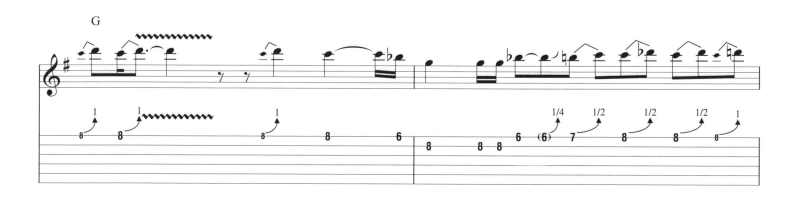

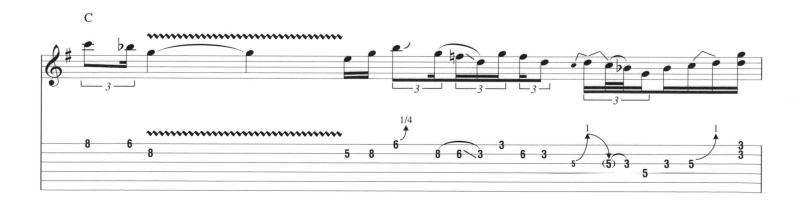

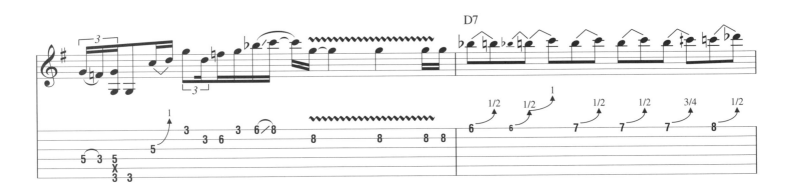

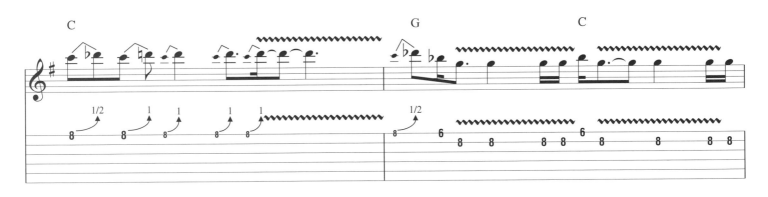

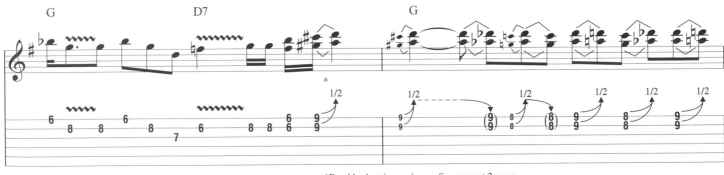

*Bend both strings w/ same finger, next 2 meas.

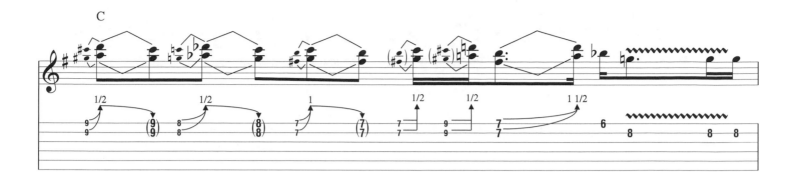

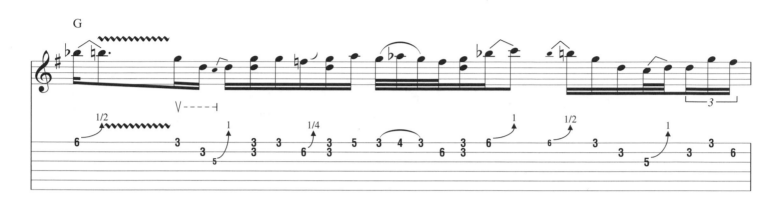

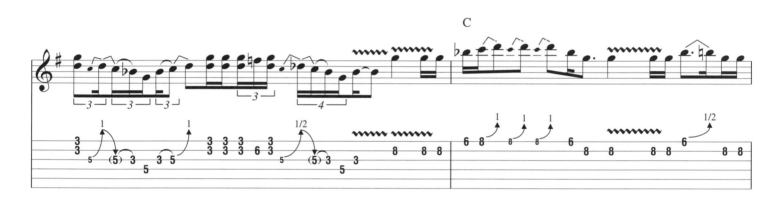

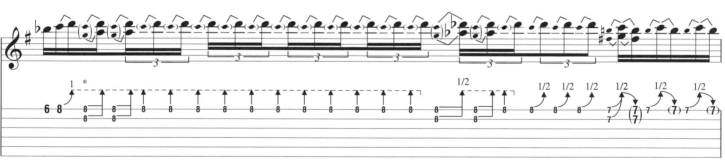

*As before, this measure only.

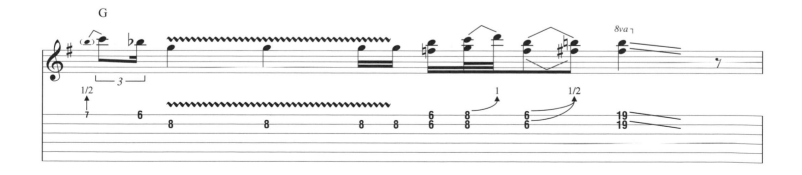

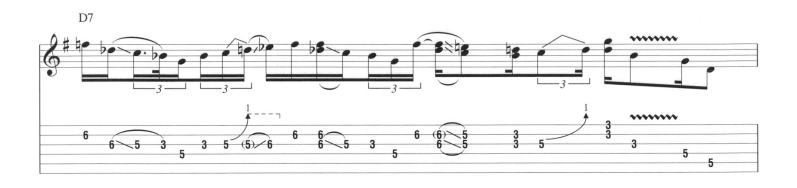

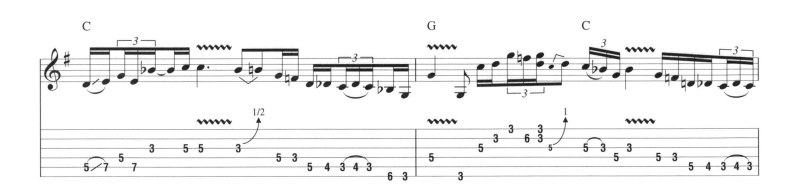

3. Well, __ I'm leav-in' you, ba - by. _____

Lord, ___ now I'm go-in' back home ___ to stay.

Well, _____ I'm ___

leav - in' you, ba - by. _____

Lord, _____ 'n' I'm go - in' back home to stay.

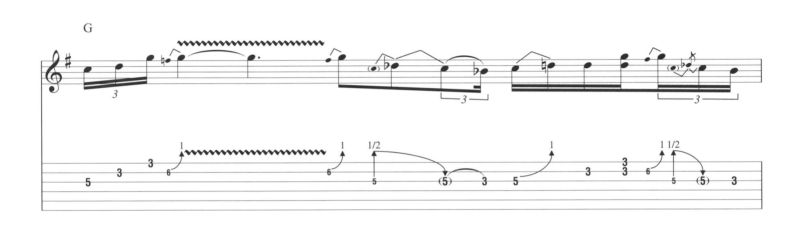

G

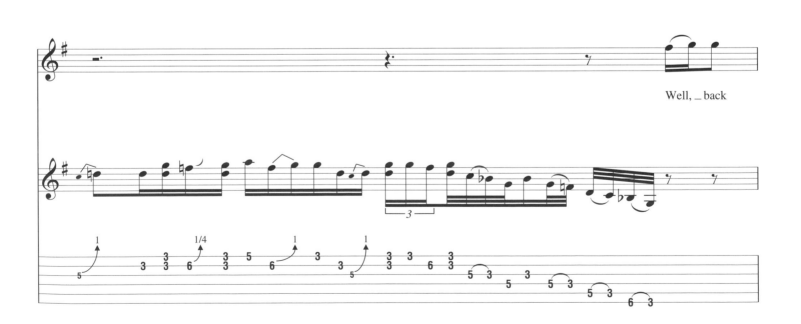

Well, _ back

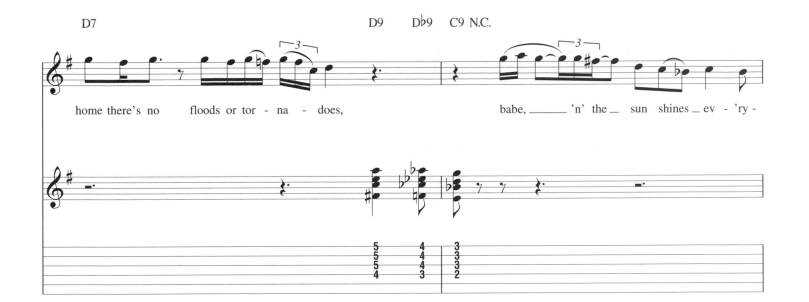

home there's no   floods or tor - na - does,   babe, _____ 'n' the _ sun shines _ ev - 'ry-

Free time

day. _____

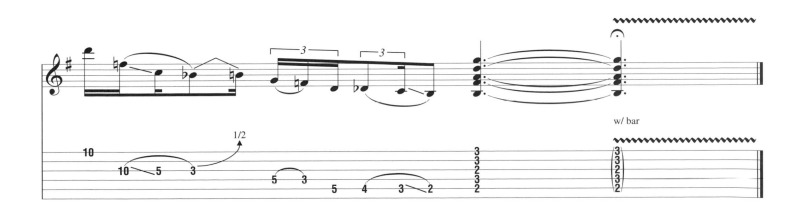

w/ bar

THE THRILL IS GONE
B.B. King

Video Lesson – 18 minutes, 48 seconds

Standard Tuning: (low to high) E–A–D–G–B–E
Key of B minor

Guitar Tone:

- light distortion

- bridge pickup

- EQ: bass – 5, mid – 6, treble – 7

Scales:

B Minor Pentatonic Scale

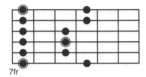

7fr

B.B. Box (Variation)

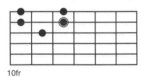

10fr

Techniques:

- String Bending: as in most blues, string bending is a must-know technique. Be sure to keep your bend pitches in tune! Practice these by fretting the target pitches first to hear how far you should bend the strings to nail the proper pitches.

- 1st-Finger Bends: there are many bends in this song that are played with the 1st finger, which can prove difficult because of the lack of support fingers behind it. Work on strengthening your 1st finger so you can execute these bends with authority. As an alternative, you can fret them with your middle finger instead, gaining the 1st finger for support.

- Pre-Bends: For a pre-bend, the string is bent up to the target pitch *before* it is picked. The trick is to bend the string the correct distance without actually hearing it. Practice pre-bends by fretting the target pitches first to hear how far you should bend the strings, then follow this by attempting the pre-bend. Eventually, you'll be able to feel the right tension.

- Vibrato: defined as a repeated fluctuation of pitch, vibrato is typically used on notes of a longer duration. It is achieved by bending and releasing a string over and over. B.B. King was known for his "butterfly" vibrato—a quick, subtle shake with his index finger on 2nd-string notes, in which his hand resembles the rapid flutter of a butterfly's wings, anchored only by the crook of his index finger. Bent notes are also treated with vibrato. First, bend the note to the desired pitch, then shake the string from this point (slightly bending above and/or below the position of the bent note).

- Staccato: notes with a dot over them indicate staccato. This means they should be cut short and not allowed to ring out. After the initial attack, use your left and right hands to mute the strings.

The Thrill Is Gone

Words and Music by Roy Hawkins and Rick Darnell

Intro
Moderately slow Blues ♩ = 88

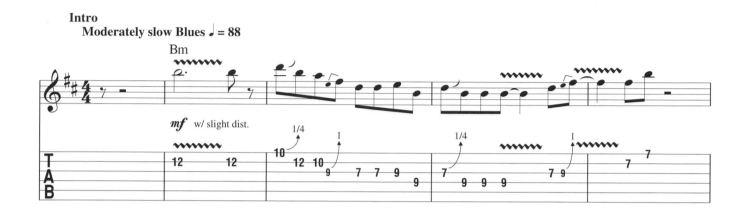

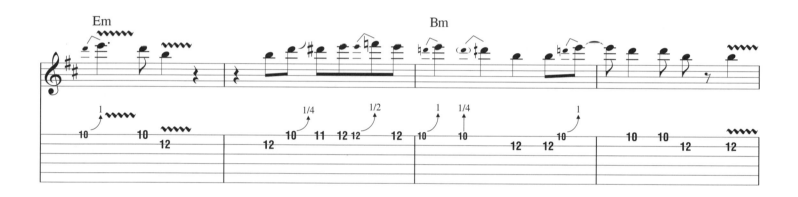

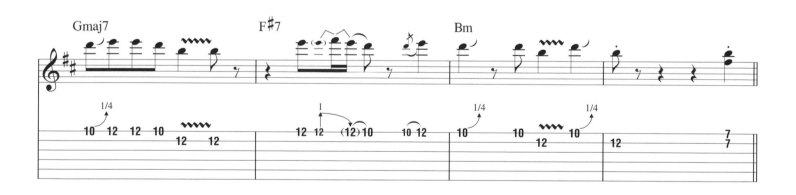

1. The thrill is gone,___ the thrill is gone a - way.___
3. *See additional lyrics*

The thrill is gone,____ ba - by, the thrill is gone____

____ a - way.____ You know you done me wrong,____ ba -

To Coda ⊕

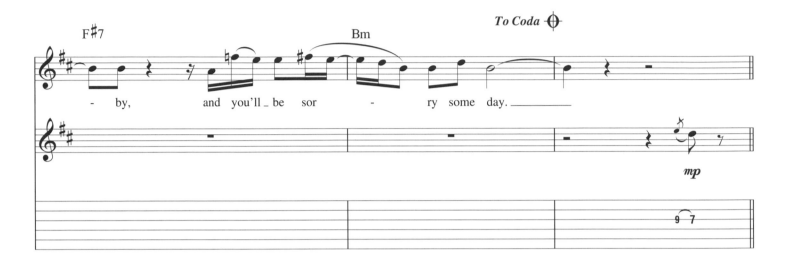

- by, and you'll _ be sor - ry some day.____

mp

Verse

2. The thrill is gone, it's gone a - way _ from me.____

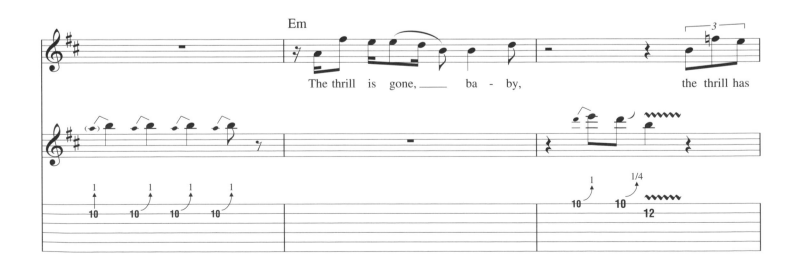

The thrill is gone,____ ba - by, the thrill has

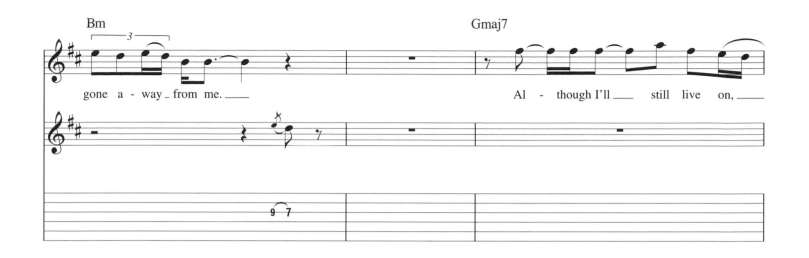

gone a - way from me. ____ Al - though I'll ____ still live on, ____

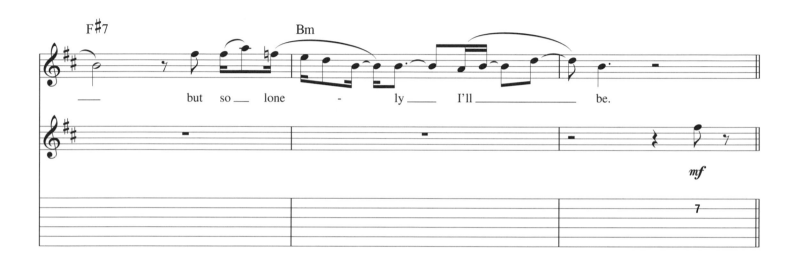

____ but so ____ lone - ly ____ I'll ____ be.

Guitar Solo

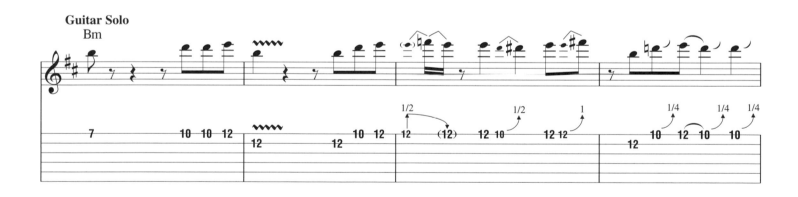

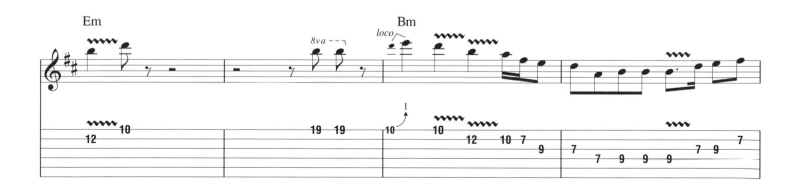

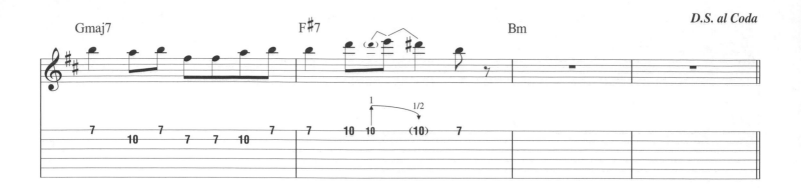

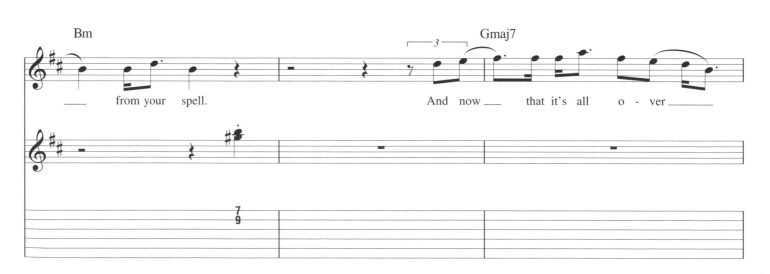

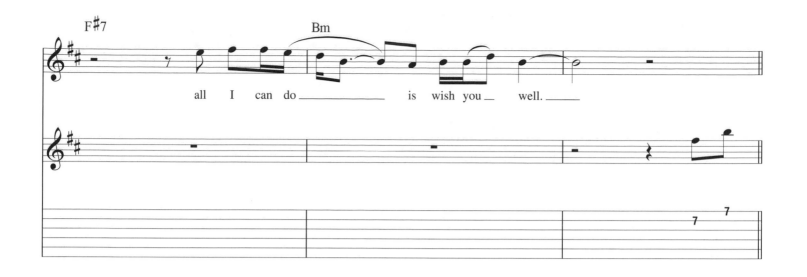

all I can do _____ is wish you_ well. _____

Outro-Guitar Solo

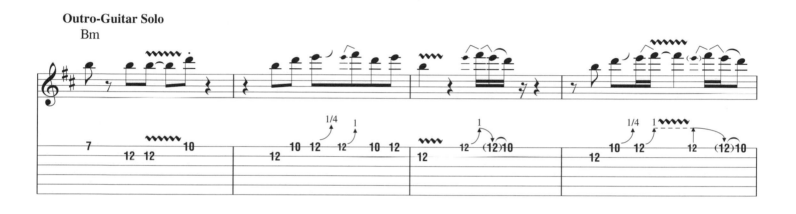

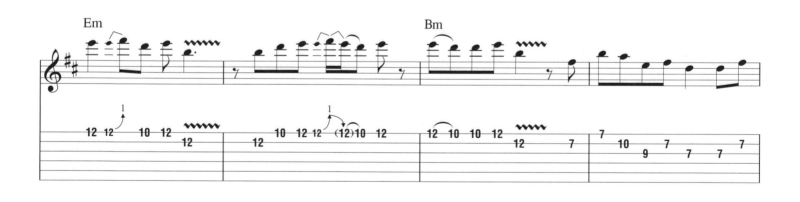

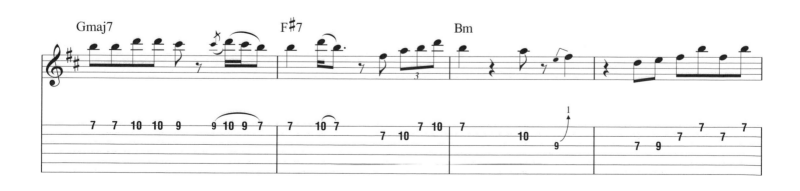

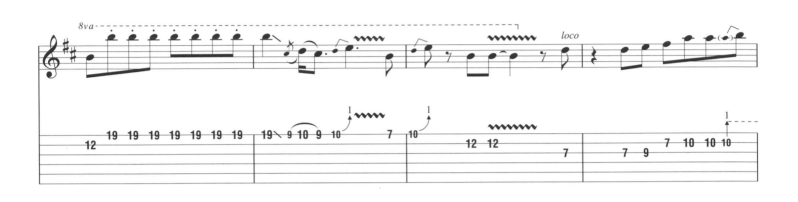

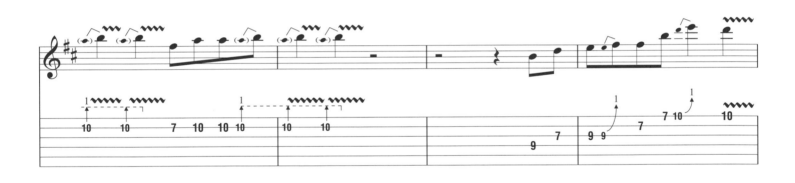

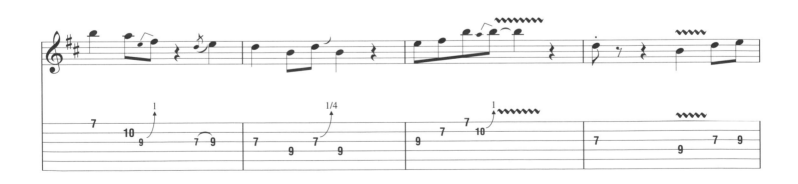

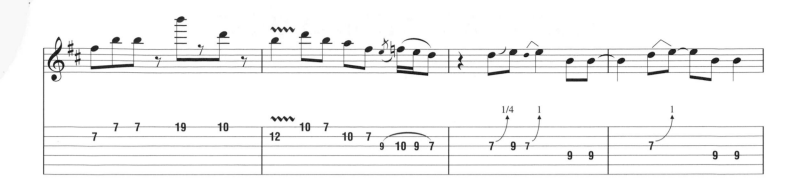

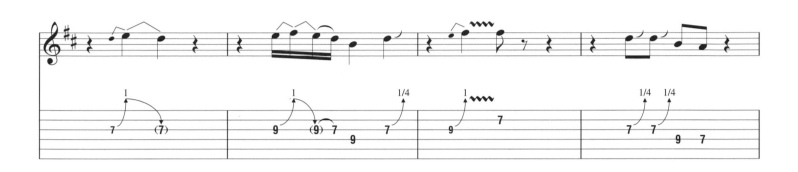

Begin fade

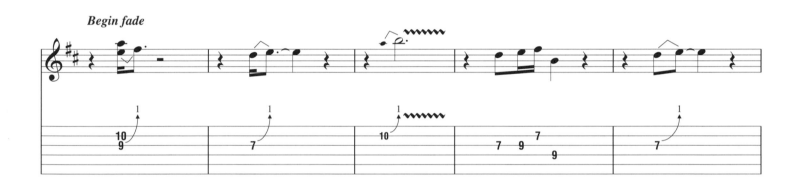

Fade out

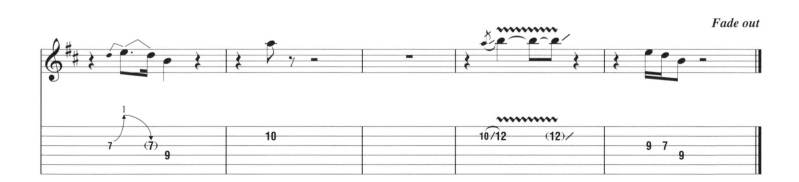

Additional Lyrics

3. The thrill is gone,
   It's gone away for good.
   Oh, the thrill is gone,
   Baby, it's gone away for good.
   Someday I know I'll be holdin' on, baby,
   Just like I know a good man should.

GUITAR NOTATION LEGEND

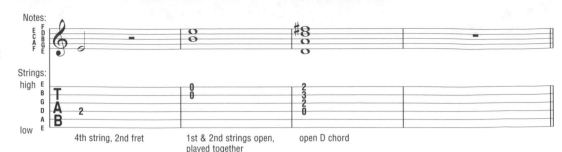

THE MUSICAL STAFF shows pitches and rhythms and is divided by bar lines into measures. Pitches are named after the first seven letters of the alphabet.

TABLATURE graphically represents the guitar fingerboard. Each horizontal line represents a string, and each number represents a fret.

4th string, 2nd fret   1st & 2nd strings open, played together   open D chord

HALF-STEP BEND: Strike the note and bend up 1/2 step.

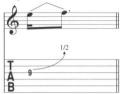

WHOLE-STEP BEND: Strike the note and bend up one step.

GRACE NOTE BEND: Strike the note and immediately bend up as indicated.

SLIGHT (MICROTONE) BEND: Strike the note and bend up 1/4 step.

BEND AND RELEASE: Strike the note and bend up as indicated, then release back to the original note. Only the first note is struck.

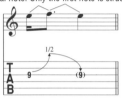

PRE-BEND: Bend the note as indicated, then strike it.

VIBRATO: The string is vibrated by rapidly bending and releasing the note with the fretting hand.

PALM MUTING: The note is partially muted by the pick hand lightly touching the string(s) just before the bridge.

HAMMER-ON: Strike the first (lower) note with one finger, then sound the higher note (on the same string) with another finger by fretting it without picking.

PULL-OFF: Place both fingers on the notes to be sounded. Strike the first note and without picking, pull the finger off to sound the second (lower) note.

LEGATO SLIDE: Strike the first note and then slide the same fret-hand finger up or down to the second note. The second note is not struck.

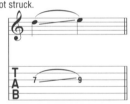

SHIFT SLIDE: Same as legato slide, except the second note is struck.

TRILL: Very rapidly alternate between the notes indicated by continuously hammering on and pulling off.

TAPPING: Hammer ("tap") the fret indicated with the pick-hand index or middle finger and pull off to the note fretted by the fret hand.

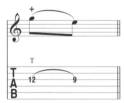

NATURAL HARMONIC: Strike the note while the fret-hand lightly touches the string directly over the fret indicated.

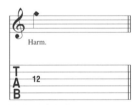

PINCH HARMONIC: The note is fretted normally and a harmonic is produced by adding the edge of the thumb or the tip of the index finger of the pick hand to the normal pick attack.

TREMOLO PICKING: The note is picked as rapidly and continuously as possible.

VIBRATO BAR DIVE AND RETURN: The pitch of the note or chord is dropped a specified number of steps (in rhythm), then returned to the original pitch.

VIBRATO BAR SCOOP: Depress the bar just before striking the note, then quickly release the bar.

VIBRATO BAR DIP: Strike the note and then immediately drop a specified number of steps, then release back to the original pitch.

Additional Musical Definitions

(accent) • Accentuate note (play it louder).

(staccato) • Play the note short.

D.S. al Coda • Go back to the sign (𝄋), then play until the measure marked "*To Coda*," then skip to the section labelled "*Coda*."

D.C. al Fine • Go back to the beginning of the song and play until the measure marked "*Fine*" (end).

Fill • Label used to identify a brief melodic figure which is to be inserted into the arrangement.

N.C. • Harmony is implied.

• Repeat measures between signs.

• When a repeated section has different endings, play the first ending only the first time and the second ending only the second time.